The Fears of Childhood

The Fears of Childhood

A Guide to Recognizing and Reducing Fearful States in Children

Edward P. Sarafino, Ph.D.

Trenton State College
Department of Psychology
Trenton, New Jersey

 HUMAN SCIENCES PRESS, INC.
72 FIFTH AVENUE
NEW YORK, N.Y. 10011

Published by Human Sciences Press, Inc.
72 Fifth Avenue, New York, New York 10011

Printed in the United States of America
987654321

Library of Congress Cataloging in Publication Data

Sarafino, Edward P.
  The fears of childhood.

  Bibliography: p. 206
  Includes index
  1. Fear in children. I. Title.
BF723.F4S27   1985   155.4′12   85-8045
ISBN 0-89885-249-8
      0-89885-296-X (paperback)

Contents

Acknowledgments

I feel a sense of gratitude to many people. My friends and colleagues contributed suggestions on the manuscript—especially Professor J. W. Armstrong, who read it and provided useful criticisms. Norma Fox, Editor-in-Chief at Human Sciences Press, recognized the need for this book and offered constructive advice. Trenton State College provided a grant that supported part of the effort that went into this work. Acknowledgments also go to (a) my typist, Joanne Vanisko, (b) students and parents who helped clarify my ideas about the development of fears, and (c) the children whose fears I have used as examples. Lastly, I thank my family and close friends whose support and confidence girded me against anxiety and enabled me to take on many challenges. This book is dedicated to them.

A Note from the Author

Because most of the cases described in this book are based on actual incidents, I have tried to maintain anonymity of the people in two ways. First, I never used the real surname of a character, and first names were typically changed. Second, I altered some aspects of incidents and characters, such as the person's age or gender.

Preface

If you feel a responsibility to help a child be happier and suffer less fear, this book is written for you. Whether you are—or expect to be—a parent, or a teacher, or another child-care provider, you'll find this book useful. It contains many tried-and-true methods and ideas for helping children cope with fear.

What's "special" about *this* book? There are many books that give advice about child-rearing and children's problems. *This* book gives you *straightforward and practical information that you can apply* directly when childhood fears arise. Better still, it tells you specific ways you can help *prevent* fears from developing. And if a child has one or more fears that you suspect may be too serious for you to handle, this book describes signs to help you decide whether your suspicions are correct and provides advice on seeking professional help. I have given many examples throughout the book to make concepts and methods come to life.

In the first chapters, we'll look at what fears are and what children fear at different ages. Then we'll consider "where fears come from"—inborn sources of fear, the impact of the child's experiences, and how thinking and imagination play a role in making the child fearful. Finally, the lion's share of the book describes useful methods to prevent and reduce fears, focusing on the many common worries of childhood. And as you read this book, you'll find answers to many questions you may have. Why are some children more fearful than others? Why do some fears persist and get worse? If I do nothing, will the child outgrow fears? Are there games and children's books the child and I can share together that can help this child cope with fears?

There is one more thing I should say. Remember that each child is unique and each fear is different. You know a lot about the child you want to help—a lot more than I do, since I've never met that child. The methods I describe are those that have worked for other children. Use my ideas as a guide, not a strict formula or prescription. If you are caring and responsive to the child's needs, I'm confident you'll use this guide effectively. And that will satisfy my most hopeful goal in writing this book.

1

The Textures of Fear

JIMMY, JO, AND PAT

When Jimmy and his mother walked through the door-
way marked Dr. Johnson, DDS, it was Jimmy's first visit
to the dentist. The pleasant receptionist greeted him saying, "You must be Jimmy. That's a handsome coat you're
wearing. How old are you?"

"I'm almost four years old," he answered, groping for
his mother's hand.

"Well," she continued, "we have lots of nice picture
books you can look at while you wait."

Jimmy and his mother sat on the sofa looking at books,
and after a while the receptionist said, "The dentist will be
ready for you in a minute, Jimmy." His body tensed a bit,
and he snuggled closer to his mother.

"Are you afraid, Jimmy?" his mother asked.

"No. I'm not afraid, Mommy," he said as he continued
to snuggle close to her.

"Well, Jimmy, it's OK if you're afraid a little."

"I *am* afraid, Mommy. What will he do to me?"

"It's good to let me know when you're afraid," she responded, "because sometimes I can help. I'll go with you into the office and I'll be near where you can see me. Dr. Johnson is a nice man. But he has to look carefully in your mouth and put some things in there so he can see if your teeth are growing OK."

Young children are fearful of many things. Some of their fears are relatively mild, like the one Jimmy had, and the fear of doctors and dentists is fairly common in childhood. Often children will deny they are afraid of things because they have learned that they are supposed to be brave "big boys" and "big girls." Jimmy's mother realized, however, that his denial might not reveal his true feelings. She let him know that being afraid is an acceptable feeling and gave him the opportunity to reveal his concerns freely. By doing this she was then able to take steps that probably reduced the potential for a traumatic experience and avoided the development of a more intense fear.

Most children develop at least a few fears that are stronger than Jimmy's fear at the dentist's office. At five years of age Jo was a generally well-adjusted girl, but she had acquired a rather strong fear of flying insects, especially if they were large or made a buzzing noise when they flew. Her fear seemed to begin during the previous summer when she had two experiences involving flying insects. In June she saw a movie on television in which swarms of bees pursued and attacked adults and children, apparently at random and without cause. The attacks were shown in graphic detail—the victims were horrified and in great pain, writhing and flailing about. They suffered severe injuries—the swelling and discoloration of the skin shown in wonderfully vivid color—and many died.

After Jo saw this movie, she seemed wary of insects and asked a lot of questions about them. Then in July she was riding her tricycle in the back yard when she rode over a yellow jacket nest that was burrowed into the ground. Yellow jackets swarmed out in defense of their disturbed nest, and as she dismounted her tricycle and tried to escape, she received stings on her ear and arm. Her father heard the terror in Jo's screams and rushed outside to help. He quickly determined what was happening, scooped her up, and ran into the house. Although she was now protected from the yellow jackets, the traumatic event was nevertheless extended: her brother kept asking to see her "scars" and saying things like "Tommy says you can die from stings," and "Ooow, those look yecky; do they hurt a lot?" Meanwhile her parents, looking very concerned, were simultaneously trying to comfort her, yelling at her brother, and arguing over the right way to treat stings.

Jo survived these events, but not without developing an aversion to flying insects. She didn't ride her tricycle on the lawn very much after that, and when she did, she watched the ground rather than where she was going. When she saw an insect flying—even a butterfly—at some distance, she would become tense, watch intently without moving, and seek the protection of an adult if one was near. If she saw a flying insect near her, she would begin to tremble, shout, "No. Go away. I don't like you," and run in a state of panic for protection and escape. Jo never used to have nightmares, but she did now. Several times she woke up screaming that "bugs are after me" and "bugs went inside me—in from my ear where they stinged me."

Jo's fear was moderately intense and needed specific attention so that it could be reduced. Helping a child to overcome a fear like hers is usually accomplished with relatively little difficulty. In general, fears are more easily reduced if they result from specific unpleasant prior experiences and if they are isolated, rather than part of an overall pattern of fearfulness or personality disorder.

Ten-year-old Pat had a much more complicated problem

that seemed to have begun very early. As a baby, he showed poor sleeping patterns, cried often, and became upset by minor events, such as when his carriage was rocked, a stranger appeared, or diapering occurred. As he grew older, he fussed when clothing was pulled over his head, rejected new foods each time they were offered, and seemed very withdrawn and unsociable with other children.

When Pat was five, he seemed to enjoy picture books, stories, and television shows that portrayed ''monster things,'' such as goblins, ghosts, and witches. He would watch and listen with apparent delight, eyes wide open with curiosity. Soon he became very preoccupied with these creatures and would ask endless questions about them, particularly in the evening around bedtime. Then one night after going to bed, Pat noticed some strange-looking shadows all around his room, and he began to imagine that they were ghosts and goblins. He lay there motionless and breathless, afraid that stirring would call attention to him and they would ''get'' him. His heart began to beat quickly and strongly, and he became concerned that they would hear how loudly his heart was beating. His mouth became dry, his lips started to quiver, and soon his whole body was trembling. Convinced that the monsters would shortly notice him, he panicked and began screaming. When his parents rushed in, he was thrashing about wildly, and it took several minutes to calm him down. From that night on, he remained terrified of the dark and always kept a light on at night.

Pat also had problems socially and at school. He continued to be relatively shy, especially when meeting new people. He was constantly getting into fights with other children, even with the few friends he had. In class he was restless and fidgety, often wandering around the room. When the teacher reprimanded him for inappropriate behavior, he became violent, and later he would mope about for long periods of time. He worried a great deal about his ability in schoolwork, how he looked when he tried to play sports, and what people thought of him. And when he worried, he began to stutter while asking questions to gain reassurance. Exams at school and events in which he was expected to speak before a group were extremely difficult for him. Several times when events such as these were scheduled, he became physically ill and had to be sent home from school. Clearly, Pat had many serious fears that he could not cope with and that were impairing his social and psychological development.

The cases of Jimmy, Jo, and Pat describe different types and intensities of children's fears. We will return to these cases to illustrate points and concepts several times in this chapter.

What Are Fears, When Are They Problems?

We all experience the feeling of fear at one time or other. *Fear* is a normal emotional response to a perceived threat that may be real or imagined. The feeling we have is a combination of *psychological discomfort,* such as wariness, worry, apprehension, or horror, and *physical arousal,* such as increased heart rate or perspiration.

The feeling of fear is a protective and adaptive response that alerts us to danger and thereby helps us to survive. Self-preservation and protection against harm are basic forces in adaptive human behavior. Children who fall into a large body of water will not simply allow themselves to sink. Sensing danger, they will make an effort toward survival: they will call for help, swim if they know how, or do whatever else they can to stay afloat.

Children learn many important things from the experiences they have in their worlds, one of which is to *antici- pate* danger. This anticipation arouses fear and motivates children to be cautious and prudent, and this prevents them from being harmed. Children who have learned about the potential dangers of fast-moving cars are likely to cross streets carefully, looking both ways and waiting for the green light. The fear most children experience in crossing streets is only enough to produce cautious behavior. Intense fear might prevent children from crossing streets at all, and this would not be useful. But children who do not anticipate the potential dangers of certain situations may find themselves burned from playing with matches, cut by an improperly handled knife, bitten because they pull a dog's tail too hard, hospitalized after a serious fall from a window, kidnapped after accepting a ride from a stranger, or worse.

Human behavior is not guided simply by objectively experienced events—the way each person *perceives* an event is also important. If a group of people were to witness a robbery, each person's description of the event would be somewhat different from that of the other witnesses. This would occur partly because each person's attention might have been focused on different aspects of the situation, but also because our perception is influenced by what we have learned in the past and what we expect to see. One witness might say that the victim "looked terrified," but others might say he "looked angry" or even "looked calm," depending on their expectations and past experience.

Similarly, some children perceive themselves to be threatened—that is, they feel fear—when other children in the same situation do not. Whether or not a child's reaction should be considered a "problem" is determined by the intensity of the fear response, the degree of real danger, how persistent the fear has been, and the extent to which the reaction interferes with normal physical, social, and intellectual growth. Underreacting by not perceiving a dangerous situation as threatening can be as much of a problem as overreacting.

Imagine that Ginny, Vicki, and Elly are boarding a roll-ercoaster. Ginny is a bit tense, but that's a normal reaction and it leads her to make sure the safety bar is positioned and functioning correctly. However, Vicki perceives no threat at all. As we have already seen, not perceiving a dangerous situation as threatening can be a problem—and Vicki's underreaction leads her to try doing some "stunts" while the ride is operating. In contrast, Elly's reaction is one of great terror. Her overreaction is dangerous because she fails to check the safety bar and she becomes totally panicked as the ride ascents the first peak. Fortunately, the safety bar did lock and Ginny could comfort her to the end of the ride.

The cases of Jimmy, Jo, and Pat that were described earlier are useful in making some distinctions about fears. Jimmy's mild fear of what the dentist would do to him was both normal and reasonable. It was his first dental exami-nation, and the things that would be done were unclear to him. The examination procedure had not yet been ex-plained and, as far as he knew, it might hurt. His mother noticed the subtle signs of fear and took steps that could help prevent the fear from becoming much stronger. "An ounce of prevention" is always preferable to dealing with an intense fear later on.

Jo's fear of flying insects was rather strong. She was afraid of virtually all flying insects—including many that could not harm her—and she would tremble and run away in fright. Although you could say that it is reasonable to react with fear to potentially harmful insects, such as wasps and bees, her reaction was excessive; wariness and mild avoidance of a nearby wasp would be appropriate, panic would not. Jo's fear can be called a phobia. *Phobias* are intense and irrational fears that are directly associated with specific events and situations. Some children are afraid of being enclosed in small rooms, and are described as claus-trophobic. Other common phobias involve the fear of darkness, animals, high places, thunderstorms, and school.

In Jo's case, except for her insect phobia, she was a cheerful, happy, and well-adjusted little girl. Pat, on the other hand, was an unhappy child who had poor social relationships and suffered from many fears. His intense fears of monsters and darkness qualify as phobias, and he had frequent anxieties about social relationships and schoolwork. *Anxiety* is a vague feeling of uneasiness or apprehension—a gloomy anticipation of impending doom—that has a relatively uncertain or unspecific source. That is, the child may not be aware either of which situations seem to arouse anxiety or of what the "doom" entails. Pat's anxieties over exams and events where he would have to speak in public were debilitating, and even made him physically ill. Anxieties are often tied to feelings of low self-worth and the anticipation of a loss of either self-esteem or the esteem of others.

Are fears, phobias, and anxieties basically the same thing? In a sense, yes, they are, since they all involve a disquieting emotional state that is based upon a feeling of threat. The term *fear* includes both *phobia* (an intense and irrational fear of something specific) and *anxiety* (a fear that has a vague or unspecific source). Some writers make a distinction between anxiety and fear, claiming that a fear has a specific source. But the *Webster's New Collegiate Dictionary* (1976) uses each term to define the other, and distinctions between fear and anxiety often are not useful in practice.[1] As a result, I will use the term *fear* interchangeably with phobia and anxiety, while distinguishing between the two latter terms as different kinds of fears.

Would the fears of Jimmy, Jo, and Pat *all* be considered "problems"? No, of course not. Certainly Pat's fears were the most serious and would qualify as problems that were impairing his social and intellectual development. Fears as serious as his generally require professional therapy. But Jo's phobia for flying insects was a less serious problem, and Jimmy's wariness at the dentist's office was actually an appropriate reaction. Fears like these two can be helped —and more serious fears can be avoided—by the actions of careful and sensitive nontherapists, such as parents and teachers. Psychologists have developed several useful and straightforward methods that *you* can apply to help a child overcome fears and prevent them from becoming serious problems.

At this point you may be wondering about several important questions, such as:

What are the methods I can use to help a child cope with fears?

Are there things that parents do that make the child's fear worse?

What if I do nothing about the fear—will it get worse?

How do I know whether a fearful child needs professional therapy?

What causes a child to develop "problem" fears?

These and many other questions will be answered in this book, and clear-cut suggestions will be given for preventing and reducing many specific fears that occur quite commonly in childhood.

2

What Do Children Fear?

Each child develops his or her own individual set of fears. We cannot say in advance which specific fears a child will acquire—one toddler may be afraid of loud noises, while another is not. But we do know that some types of fears are more likely to develop in the early childhood years, and other fears are more likely later. We also know that girls seem to be more fearful than boys, and we will look at this issue before considering the child's age.

The Child's Age and Gender

Studies by psychologists have generally found that girls report having a greater number of fears and more intense fears than boys do.[2] Does this mean that girls are born with a greater susceptibility to fears, resulting from biological differences between boys and girls? Although this is possible, there is no evidence that it is true. What seems more likely is that the differences in fears between boys and girls result from their different experiences. Our society in general prescribes as acceptable different behaviors for boys than for girls. Boys are expected to behave in a "masculine" way—strong, unemotional, logical, adventurous, and rough-and-tumble. Girls are usually given more latitude, and it is far more acceptable for them to show emotion and weakness and to cry when upset. Children begin to learn these distinctions at a very early age from their parents, teachers, other children, and television.[3]

How do the different experiences of boys and girls affect the fears they report? For one thing girls probably feel more freedom to *admit* to having fears when asked. Second, our culture prompts girls to develop more fears by providing more restrictions and warnings about dangerous situations. Girls are more likely to be warned of the dangers involved in climbing trees or swimming, for example. Third, because a girl's fears are often more acceptable to her parents than a boy's would be, she may receive more comfort and soothing when afraid. Boys are less likely to get such consolation. Their fears are often frowned upon as "sissy" behavior, and they are admonished to be "a big boy"—or even "a man!" Finally, if the anxieties of boys are hidden behind the brave facade they are taught to present the world, their fears should show up in a different way. Perhaps the fact that boys greatly outnumber girls in childhood problems, such as stuttering, asthma, and bedwetting, reveals their hidden anxieties. These problems are either produced or intensified by emotional stress. When boys cover up their feelings by not showing their fears, their anxieties may simply be expressed in other ways.

The *types* of fears that children have are related to their age.[4] Why? One reason is that the experiences children have change as they grow older. Infants typically lead relatively quiet and isolated lives. They sleep a great deal, spend most of their waking time in their homes among familiar people, and have very few negative experiences with dogs, insects, and the like. Children in the preschool years lead very different lives. Their greatly expanded worlds, ability to get around without help, and high activity levels bring them in contact with many situations that have the potential for producing fear. But preschoolers don't only acquire fears by suffering negative situations directly—they also receive warnings about possible dangers, such as in leaning out of windows or putting fingers in electric outlets, and they learn about monsters and the like from stories, picture books, and television. Once children enter school, they begin to worry about their schoolwork, getting hurt or humiliated by bullies, and rejection by schoolmates and teachers.

Another reason the types of fears change as children get older is that their ability to think and use language increases. The fears of infants and toddlers usually arise in response to tangible and immediate events, but preschoolers' fears tend to become less concrete and more abstract. They are able to dwell on past events and think about what could happen in the future—and their fantasy life is very rich, sometimes making it difficult for them to distinguish between real and unreal events and people. As a result, children between two and six years of age become increasingly fearful of the dark, being alone, and imaginary creatures, such as ghosts or witches. Fear of animals seems to be most prevalent during the early childhood years, and is usually gone by adolescence.

Which fears are the most likely ones to occur in infancy, the preschool years, and beyond? The remainder of this chapter answers this question and describes the fears at each age level. Of course, although certain fears are most prevalent during specific age ranges, each child is unique— we cannot say which particular child will develop which fear or that a specific fear cannot occur at another age.

FEARS IN INFANCY AND TODDLERHOOD

You've probably witnessed a scene like this: a mother picks up her nine-month-old son, Neil, from his crib to meet his uncle who has just returned home after many months. The baby stares at this stranger for a while, and then he starts to cry and cling to his mother. The uncle is surprised by this reception—after all, he is sort of average-looking and he was acting in a pleasant manner. Why did Neil react with fear? Part of the answer seems to lie in the *unfamiliarity* of this person, and Neil's reaction is called "fear of strangers."

We all tend to be somewhat wary of new things, situations, and people. When you meet someone socially for the first time, you are more reserved and careful of what you say and do than you probably will be as your acquaintanceship or friendship develops. You don't yet "trust" this person, and you might be concerned about offending him or her, for instance. In early infancy, babies begin to form close bonds of love and trust with important and familiar people in their lives, especially with their parents. Babies also form a mental picture of the faces of these important people.

Neil had accomplished this, and the bond he felt toward his mother was very strong. He sometimes even showed distress when he saw her wearing unfamiliar dark glasses, a new hairdo, or a hat. Not all infants are fearful of strangers, but they are more likely to be if they have had very little social contact with people outside the immediate family, if they encounter this stranger in an unfamiliar place, such as a new doctor's waiting room, and if their parents are not present when the stranger appears. Infants who develop a fear of strangers generally do so sometime between five and twelve months of age.[5] After the first year, the fear reaction to strangers usually fades but may be transformed into a shyness around new people.

Another fear that infants commonly develop after six months of age is called "separation distress."[6] This is the fear that babies and young children show when left alone by the persons whom the child has come to know, love, and trust—once again, the parents. Everyday short-term separations seem to produce relatively mild reactions, particularly if the child is in a familiar place. Once infants are able to get around, even by crawling and creeping, they pursue their mothers around the house, following from room to room. When they are alone, but know their mothers are not very far away and can be reached, infants can usually explore and play comfortably even in an unfamiliar environment.

What happens if one-year-olds are left alone for several minutes in an unfamiliar environment and they cannot follow their mothers? They usually show signs of distress— sometimes only a mild disquietude, but more often the distress is much stronger: they begin to cry and scream, and try to find their mothers. They go to the door, try to open it, and bang on it. When they finally give up this approach, some busy themselves in play or exploration of the room but others are so distressed that they simply sit with a troubled expression on their faces and rock back and forth. The reaction of these children to Mother when she returns also shows the anxiety they felt. They stay closer to her than usual, touching her and looking at her frequently.

Brief separations like this are not uncommon, and children need to become accustomed to these situations eventually if, for example, they are to attend nursery school. But what happens to children when long-term separation occurs? Prolonged hospitalization, abandonment, or orphaning can produce very severe distress in the child, and the reaction goes through three phases: *protest, despair,* and *detachment*.[7] The separation distress suffered by a girl named Dolores illustrates these phases. When she entered the hospital at twenty months of age, her parents could not visit her very often because the hospital was far from where they lived. Her initial distress was shown in her crying, frequent calling for "Mommy," and trying to climb out of her crib.

During the next day, Dolores's protest reaction began to wane and after a while she became very quiet and withdrawn. Now reacting with despair, her infrequent cries had a monotonous and hopeless tone. She slept poorly, had little appetite, and seemed miserable, inconsolable, and listless. Eventually her mood became more "normal," and she began to accept the attention and care of the nurses and physicians. Dolores *seemed* to have "gotten over it," but she was not really "back to normal"—she had reached the phase of detachment, when the characteristic response is indifference. When her parents were able to visit, she liked the presents they brought but she had very little interest in *them* as important people. She seemed no longer to trust or care for anyone. When she returned home after her one-month stay, she was difficult, bad-tempered, and clinging for the next several weeks.

Although not all children show this degree of disturbance,[8] long-term separation distress often takes this form. Children between six months and four years of age are most likely to be fearful of separation and react in this way. Children who are apt to be most fearful are those who are in the hospital with painful injuries or operations, have not visited or stayed overnight in other peoples' houses, and who already have many fears and anxieties or come from unhappy homes.

Other fears that infants and toddlers develop stem from their inborn fright reaction to pain, sudden loud noises, bright lights, and loss of physical support, as in falling. It was in this manner that a little boy named Tony acquired an unusual fear: red doors. The first time his mother noticed this fear they were entering the home of a relative, but she couldn't figure out what had frightened him. She didn't realize that it was the red door on the house that produced his distress. One doesn't come across many red doors, and so Tony's fear was not tested again until a few weeks later when they were entering a store that had a red door. Once again, his mother was perplexed by his distress.

Then when Tony was eighteen months old, he and his mother went to the pediatrician's office for his scheduled vaccinations. As they approached the medical building, Tony began crying and screaming "No go. No go." It was at that moment that his mother noticed that the entry had a red door, and the doors at the relative's house and the store flashed into her mind. She also remembered that this was the same place Tony had gotten his two-, four-, six-, and twelve-month vaccinations, and where he had received a series of painful treatments a few months ago. Children—even infants—can associate things they notice (in this case, a red door) as "signals" of possible threat or danger.

FEARS IN THE PRESCHOOL AND EARLY SCHOOL YEARS

We have seen that certain fears tend to decline in early childhood while new fears emerge. One fear that usually retains its prominence during these years is separation distress, and it frequently underlies two common childhood problems: *school phobia* and *death phobia*.

School phobia is an intense fear related to attending school that often begins when the child starts preschool or kindergarten. For most children this transition can be rather abrupt, and they must adapt to many changes in their social worlds. In this unfamiliar place, they meet many new children and have to learn how to interact with them. Perhaps more important is that there are new adults to care for them—Mommy and Daddy are not there. "Will these new adults be nice?" the child may worry, especially if this translates into: "Can I trust these strangers to treat me well, care for me if I get hurt, comfort me when I'm unhappy, and provide for my basic needs?"

Some children sail through this transition with little or no problem, but most feel at least a moderate degree of apprehension. Those who become school phobic typically resist staying in school or try to avoid going to school. They may ask their parents to keep them home and, when this doesn't work, try more compelling approaches, such as begging, crying, pathetically pleading, or having a tantrum. Sometimes they will offer reasons for staying home: school phobic children may (1) describe problems at school, such as being afraid of teachers or classmates; (2) claim that special difficulties await them on the way to school, such as snarling dogs; or (3) feign illness. In some cases they even show physical symptoms of illness—the child may be flushed or even vomiting.

Obviously these symptoms of illness do not always indicate that the child is school phobic. Children really *do* become ill, of course—some more than others. But if, for example, the child complains of illness often, recovers miraculously after an hour or so when allowed to stay home, and almost never complains of illness on nonschool days, school phobia may be the problem.

Sometimes the child's reluctance to go to school is related to real difficulties and dangers at or on the way to school. You can determine this fairly straightforwardly and, if necessary, the problems should be addressed. But in most cases the underlying cause of school phobias in early childhood relates—at least in part—to the feelings that the child and parents have about each other. In these cases, the child and parent—usually the mother—appear to have a mutually dependent relationship, and separation is disturbing to both. One study of this interdependent relationship was made with nursery-school children who were already showing anxiety problems as they started to attend school.

The mother-child behavior was described in the following way.

> During the first days, a typical child would remain close to mother and then begin to oscillate toward and away from attractions of the play area. As the child began to look less at mother and more away from her, she would take a seat closer to the child and occasionally use a pretext of wiping his nose or checking his toilet needs for intruding into the child's activity. Separation was as difficult for the mother as it was for the child.[9]

Parents who have difficulty with separation from their child may convey their anxiety through overprotectiveness, fussing over the child, and trembling reassurances that "everything will be fine" at school. During early childhood, children become increasingly attuned to signs of fear in others.

If a child develops a *death phobia* in early childhood, it is probably related to separation distress. Most of us feel uneasy and somewhat anxious about the possibility that we, or a loved one, might die soon. However, a child who is phobic about death becomes increasingly preoccupied with this fear and may be obsessed with concerns that one or both parents will die. This is not "wishful thinking" by the child—it is a fear of being left alone without the care, protection, and love of the parents. Sometimes the child will become so fearful that he or she will follow the mother around the house constantly in an effort to keep her in sight, if not touch.

A conception of what death is involves highly abstract thinking. As a result, death is not well understood by a young child. Important changes in the concept of death take place between three and ten years of age.[10] At first children consider death to be like living in another place. Therefore, it is a reversible process; the person can come back. Even if they know that the deceased was buried in a coffin, three- or four-year-old children usually think the person still breathes, eats, sleeps, and plays. This is why you will hear young children say things like: "If Danny is dead, will his mommy still let him play with me?" and "Dead people don't like you to make noise. They get mad when you wake them up." The drawing by four-year-old Freddie, shown in Figure 1, depicts his notion that a dead man can ride a horse.

Where do children get such notions? Probably from adults who try to "spare" the child from understanding the realities of death. They tell the child that the dead person "has gone away," or "is in Heaven, with Jesus," or "is only sleeping." Children also see "dead" people come back to life on television or hear about such things in children's stories. But even if you were to give a four-year-old careful and patient explanations of death as a concept, some of the ideas probably would be too abstract to "sink in." Abstract concepts are extremely difficult for young children to grasp.

Young children also do not usually think of death as inevitable. They may say that "you don't have to die," envisioning that death can be avoided. This idea may be especially likely if they begin to picture death as a monster, as many children do at age five or six. These children will argue that "You won't die if you run faster than the monster or trick it." After this time, children begin to understand that death happens to everyone eventually, but they may continue to have vivid ideas of death as a monster. The highly imaginative drawings of two eight-year-old boys depict these ideas in Figures 2 and 3.

Between six and ten years of age, children show a gradual increase in their understanding that death is final and that it involves an absence of bodily functions: "People who are dead can't hear or see anymore." In contrast to the younger child who views death as abandonment or

Fig. 1. Freddie (4 years, 2 months): "A horse with a dead man riding on him."

Figures 1, 2 and 3 are reprinted from *Children's Conceptions of Death*, by Richard Lonetto (pp. 54, 106, 107). Copyright © 1980 by Springer Publishing Company, Inc., New York. Used by permission.

Fig. 2. Freddie (8 years, 4 months): "Death is a guy who has one eye and one no eye, one arm and a half an arm. His hair is sticking up and he's frightening. He has a cut on his face. One half his body is brown, one half is blue, he stands on little spikes."

Fig. 3. Joey (8 years): "Death is a man with three heads. He is the person who makes you die. He is frightening and if you see him you get scared."

separation from parents, older children begin to learn that death can involve pain, injury, and disease. As a result, they may be mostly afraid of the pain and bodily injury they might suffer at the hands of the bogeyman.

By the age of ten or so, most children have the complete conception of death as an inevitable and final absence of life. Their descriptions of it include sadness and anxiety, and they no longer think of death as a monster. Their representations of death are more abstract, as eleven-year-old Jimmy wrote:

> Death is blackness . . . like when you close your eyes. It's cold and when you die your body is cold. Frightening, I don't want to die . . . I wonder then, how I'm going to die . . . I feel scared and I try to forget it. When I feel like this, I try to forget it and just put something else into my mind.[11]

When young children hear about the death of another person, their misconceptions about death may lead to fears, as in the case of seven-year-old Allen.

> His mother, who had been pregnant for six months, gave birth to a premature baby who only lived a few hours . . . When Allen's mother came home from the hospital, she told him that the baby had been too tiny and weak to live. She did not say anything about what happened to the baby's body, and Allen was too shy to ask . . . A few weeks later, Allen began to feel afraid . . . of the dark and wanted the light on in his room all night. He began to be afraid of opening a closet door or opening a dresser drawer.[12]

Later, on the advice of a psychologist, his father talked to him about the baby's death. When Allen asked what happened to the baby's body, his father described how it had been cremated. The boy felt so relieved, and he said, "I thought the baby was somewhere in the house." Small wonder that he became afraid of the dark, and of opening the closet and drawer.

In the preschool and early-school years, children seem to develop the greatest number of new fears.[13] The experiences they have in these years allow them to know so much about what things might do them harm. They have actual frightening encounters, as Jo did with yellow jackets. They also learn about the scary things that have happened to others, either among their friends, on television, or in stories. Some of the most common sources of fear in children at this time of life are listed alphabetically below.

Animals (dogs are most common) and insects
Dark (especially at bedtime)
Death (as separation, sometimes injury)
Doctors and dentists
Heights
Monsters, imaginary creatures
Nightmares
School (as separation, sometimes teachers or classmates)
Storms (and other experienced natural events)
Water (deep)

FEARS DURING MIDDLE CHILDHOOD AND ADOLESCENCE

In the early 1980s horrible stories from Atlanta began to appear in the news about the disappearance and murders of more than two dozen black children whose ages ranged from about seven to fifteen. The fears that Atlanta's children developed, as more and more bodies were discovered, serve as a gruesome introduction to this section of the book.

During the years from middle childhood to adolescence, a prominent source of fear is physical injury, particularly if severe pain or death are perceived by the child as possibilities. As the number of young victims in Atlanta mounted, pain and death became very real ''possibilities'' to the children and parents in the city's vicinity. Campaigns emerged to teach children methods of self-protection, and safety tips were distributed in leaflets at school and broadcast by radio stations throughout the day and night. Adults volunteered for special child-watching duty through many citizens' groups. Music classes in school began to teach children songs with the theme of *Kids Know No*. And sports heroes on TV were warning children to stay at home and not leave the sight of their mothers, instead of the more normal message to children: "Come on out and play. Venture forth, try things, and experience your world."

The scary-but-necessary message began getting across to parents and children: "There is a murderer out there who kills children—WATCH OUT!" Parents, adding to this message the frightening thought that "the next victim could be my child," introduced many protective measures, for instance:

One working mother required that her nine-year-old son call her at work as soon as he arrived home. The rule was, "If you don't call by 3:45 p.m., I call the police."

Parents gave children strict and detailed instructions about walking home from school, telling them to walk in groups when possible, not to talk to strangers, and what to do "if someone comes up to you and grabs you."

These are extremely stressful circumstances. Not only do parents want to protect their children from physical harm, but they also want to minimize emotional trauma for their children. What is a parent to say when a child asks, "Why does God let those kids die?" One mother answered that dying was a blessing because the children were being treated so badly. It was the only answer she could think of, but it probably fueled her son's fears—and he became withdrawn for a couple of days.

The conditions were ripe in Atlanta for the development

of fear in children: physical injury is a common worry of grade-school children, and the danger seemed very real and imminent. Serious fears swept over these children on a mass scale. Families reported to news sources that their children were showing an unusually high frequency of nightmares, bedwetting, fear of the dark, worries about being physically vulnerable, and separation problems. Children who had been fairly independent and cheerful became very clinging and resistant to doing things alone. Some children even stole knives from home to carry for self-protection and began threatening strangers who looked "suspicious." So widespread and serious was the cloud of fear that it was evidently interfering with the intellectual development of many children, according to school officials. And mental health professionals, concerned that the emotional trauma might have long-lasting effects on many children, met to discuss ways to help reduce these problems.

The development of serious childhood fears on a mass scale is unusual in recent American history. This nation has not suffered the ravages of war and famine as have other areas of the world, such as Southeast Asia, Africa, and the Middle East. As a result, the fears that children acquire pertaining to physical injury are more individualized and, although these worries are fairly common in American children, they are less likely to occur and are less intense than they could be.

What other fears are common among children from middle childhood to adolescence? Most of the new fears that children develop at this time relate to concerns about *social relationships* and individual *competence*. After children enter grade school, there are many risks that may lead to ridicule, disapproval, and rejection by parents, teachers, and age-mates. Children notice differences between each other, and they compare themselves against their classmates, using the value system of their family and society. They make comparisons of academic ability, conduct, talents, popularity, physical attractiveness, and so on. Children who see themselves as less able than their agemates begin to develop a sense of incompetence and *inferiority*.

Feelings of inferiority can sometimes involve a sense of being totally worthless—"painting" the self with broad brush strokes as "no good at anything." Although many people occasionally overreact with such broad strokes when they "mess up," for some children this sort of negative assessment of themselves becomes a characteristic or regular aspect of the self. Most children probably come to consider themselves as having a blend of strengths and weaknesses. Virtually all children and adolescents feel inferior in at least a few comparisons, and these feelings can form the foundation for shyness in social situations and anxieties about speaking in public, what clothes to buy and wear, physical and sexual attractiveness, engaging in sports, and going to school.

When school phobia develops in older children, it tends to be related to home life, school performance, or relationships with classmates. Usually the problem develops gradually—with school attendance waning over a long period of time—but sometimes the onset is fairly sudden. At the beginning of this manual I described the fears of a ten-year-old named Pat. He had social problems at school and was highly anxious in certain school-related situations, such as taking exams and speaking before a group, and these anxieties even made him physically ill. He had developed a school phobia.

In this chapter we have seen that children acquire many fears, some of which can become serious problems. The fears that are prominent at different ages were described. Knowing which fears are most prevalent at different ages is important for two reasons. First, as we shall see, you can take steps to prevent many fears from developing. And second, you can be more alert to the beginnings of fear so that you can nip them in the bud.

The descriptions of children's fears that we have seen so far gave you only a glimpse of what brings them about. For you to understand what you can do to help the child cope, we need to look more carefully at how and why fears develop—the roots of fear. This is the topic of the next two chapters.

3

The Roots of Fear

The fears that are most common in childhood, such as of separation, animals, and doctors, constitute only a small fraction of the things that the child *can* come to fear. In fact, there are almost 300 types of phobias that people have been known to develop—ranging from claustrophobia to some relatively uncommon ones, such as chronophobia (fear of clocks), asthenophobia (fear of fainting), and pteronophobia (fear of feathers).

How and why does each child develop his or her own individual set of fears? Part of the answer to this question is evident in the fears I've already described. Children *learn* fears by direct experience with negative events and by witnessing or hearing about dangers. But the roots of fear also extend into the time before the child is born. We will look at these inborn factors first.

INBORN SOURCES OF FEAR

Babies come into the world already prepared to protect themselves, as best they can, from harm. A newborn whose face is covered by a blanket will try to remove it to improve breathing—and if the blanket will not yield, the baby will struggle and begin to cry. This has obvious survival value. There is also survival value in the baby's startle or fright reaction to pain, sudden loud noises, flashes of light, and loss of physical support. All of these reactions to possible danger are inborn.

Each baby also comes into the world with certain dispositions, or basic personality characteristics, which are called *temperaments*.[14] Pediatric nurses and physicians, well aware of the unique combinations of temperaments that babies show right from birth, describe infants broadly as "easy" babies and "difficult" ones. These terms are not meant in an off-handed way—they really do describe most babies fairly accurately on the basis of differences in the way babies react to feeding, cuddling, bathing, and dressing and undressing.

"Easy" babies have a relatively smooth relationship with their worlds. They settle down to a regular schedule of sleeping, feeding, and eliminating very soon after birth. When they need attention or when changes occur in their daily routines, they make only a mild fuss and their cries are moderate in loudness and duration. These babies adapt easily to new situations and people, and their moods are predominantly pleasant and sunny.

"Difficult" babies are definitely not easy! Their daily habits are irregular—their patterns of hunger, sleep, and bowel movements are not predictable from day to day. They are not easily adaptable to new situations and people. Unlike more typical infants who begin to smile and make reaching movements when a stranger playfully shakes a rattle above them, difficult children tend to turn away, try to withdraw, and start to cry. Most changes in their routines involve a struggle and a big fuss. They cry frequently—and when they do, they tend to scream. Often when they cry, no reason for it can be found—they may refuse milk, have dry diapers, and so on—and no efforts to soothe them seem to work. On balance, difficult babies have primarily negative dispositions.

Fortunately for parents, most babies have reasonably "easy" temperaments. But a substantial proportion of children might be best described as "in between," and a fairly small proportion (about 10 percent) have clearly "difficult" temperaments. The importance of these inborn personality characteristics relates not only to the more trying experiences that parents of difficult babies can expect, but to the vulnerability of these children to developing fears. For instance, research has found that children who were classified as "difficult" were almost four times more likely than easy children eventually to enter psychiatric treatment. Difficult babies seem to be more *emotional*, and they do not cope very well with change and stress.

I do *not* want to give the impression that (1) the child's personality is "fixed" from the beginning, (2) parents play a minor role in the child's emotional development, or (3) that a difficult baby is destined to have a life filled with fear. Quite the contrary: *because the difficult baby is more vulnerable to the development of fears, the role of the parents becomes especially pivotal.*

The pivotal role of the parents is shown in the case histories of two ten-year-old boys who were difficult babies. In Sam's case, his negative disposition and irregular habits were very trying for his parents,

> . . . but they remained fond of him and together found ways of coping with the difficulties. As Sam grew older it was evident that he was a very anxious boy who found it difficult to get on with other children and who readily developed fears. There had been periods of great anxiety when his parents went out, of refusing school, of refusing to go to new places, of panic in crowds, of screaming when taken to the doctor and of fear of buses. On each occasion his parents responded with

firm and understanding encouragement and none of the problems persisted. . . . The fact that no important disorder developed was due to the warm, firm, consistent, and thoughtful
way his parents dealt with his difficulties. Temperamentally he
was a vulnerable child but he was fortunate in the life circumstances he encountered.[15]

Toby was also a difficult baby. But if we compare his
"life circumstances" with Sam's, we will see that Toby's
parents reacted quite differently.

Father was infuriated by Toby's tears and tempers and used
to hit him whenever he cried. As Toby grew older he began to
provoke his father more and the father-child relationship de-
teriorated to the point of hostility. Mother was fond of Toby
but she tended to respond to his fears by becoming increasingly worried and panicky herself so that she was unable to
help him. She had several phobias of her own and later became depressed. The end result was that Toby's difficulties
increased greatly and, when seen at age ten years, he was a
severely handicapped boy with a gross and incapacitating
emotional disorder. . . . The parents were most concerned
over Toby's worrying. He worried about school, about mother
leaving him and about meeting people. When worried, he
tended to ask endless questions, seeking reassurance but usually eliciting irritation. When he got in a panic with fear, as he
did frequently, he tended to lash out in all directions, becoming uncontrollably aggressive.[16]

Both boys were vulnerable based upon their temperaments
as babies, but Toby developed a very serious disorder and
Sam did not. Probably the contrasting ways each child's
parents dealt with their son's behavior played an important
role in the different outcomes. In Toby's case, a vicious
circle evolved in which the parent-child relationship became more and more maladaptive as his worries increased.
As we have seen, all children develop fears. Certainly

children with easy temperaments are not immune to serious problems, and not all children with difficult dispositions become highly fearful. Parents of a difficult baby can help their child by giving care that is "tender-loving" *plus* firm, consistent, patient, and understanding. Infancy is a period when this child will have an especially hard time adjusting to so many changes and new experiences: weaning to a variety of new foods; meeting new people; visiting doctors, restaurants, and stores; staying with babysitters; riding in carriages, strollers, and car safety seats; and wearing new shoes and garments. It is best to introduce the difficult baby to new situations gradually and to avoid having too many demands or changes at one time. For example, the baby would have an easier reaction to a new babysitter if they were introduced to each other gradually in the familiar surroundings of the child's home.

Why are some babies born with difficult temperaments? The reasons are not completely clear, but two factors seem to be implicated. First, there is evidence that genetics plays a role: for instance, research has shown that certain personality characteristics of difficult children are influenced by heredity, such as their emotionality. Children with a high level of emotionality tend to show "a strong temper, a tendency toward fearfulness, violent mood swings, or all of these together."[17]

The second factor relates to the mother's emotional state during pregnancy: was the pregnancy marked by an unusually high amount of stress and anxiety? Before birth, babies seem to be able to detect emotional and physical stress in their mothers. Cases have been described in which movements by the babies was heightened when the mothers were very tired and when they were experiencing fear, anxiety, or grief.[18] In one case where the mother was extremely fearful of her emotionally disturbed husband's tantrums, the baby's movements were so intense that they were described as "convulsive." Other studies of animals and humans have shown that high levels of maternal emotional stress during pregnancy can increase her offspring's emotionality *after* birth.

We do not yet understand why the baby's emotionality is affected by the factors of genetics and the mother's emotional state during pregnancy. But we do know that inborn factors play a role in the negative behaviors of most difficult babies. Many parents of these infants are quick to blame themselves and their parenting skills, thinking or saying, "I'm a terrible parent. It's my fault. I must be doing everything wrong." This is an unfair assessment that is likely to produce frustration in the parents as they try to convert a difficult baby into an easy one, and this often leads to a deterioration in the parent-child relationship. Parents of difficult babies who recognize the influence of inborn factors are more likely to deal with their vulnerable child more constructively.

EXPERIENCES AS SOURCES OF FEAR

Children—even vulnerable ones—are not born with most of the specific fears they will develop. Newborn babies are typically not afraid of the dark, monsters, animals, heights, or death, and they certainly don't worry about making a mistake while giving a speech! One way by which people acquire fears is by *direct experience with negative events*. The direct experience that Jo had with yellow jackets (Chapter 1) is a good example of how this can occur.

We all have occasional direct experiences with negative events, and these experiences sometimes instill fear. Have you ever been injured in a serious accident? Most adults probably have at some point in their lives, particularly a mishap involving automobile travel. If you have been in a car accident, you remember how you felt about automobiles and travelling in them after the accident—and the answers you might give to the following questions would reveal the extent of the fear that developed. How did you feel about:

travelling in a car, especially the same car if it was still usable, at your next opportunity to do so?

driving by "the scene of the accident" again, if you had occasion to do so?

encountering a traffic pattern or activity that is like the one at your accident, such as making a left-hand turn, coming to a stop light, or simply driving in heavy traffic?

driving in similar hazardous weather conditions, such as in snow or rain?

approaching a vehicle that looks like the one that hit yours?

Probably your fear reaction under these circumstances was at least fairly strong at first, but eventually your fear began to decline as a result of subsequent travel in cars without mishap. Many fears arise either from a single traumatic event or from repeated or sustained experience with moderately negative events. How do these experiences produce fear?

Conditioning

We *learn* from experience. Although there are several types of learning,[19] one principal way we learn fears is through *classical conditioning*—also called "respondent" or "Pavlovian" conditioning. The well-known research of the Russian physiologist Ivan Pavlov introduced the world to the way this learning process works. He was not studying fear, of course; his research was related to salivation in dogs. When food is placed in the mouth, dogs (and people!) begin to salivate as an automatic, or "reflexive," reaction. But Pavlov noticed that after the dogs had experienced the food being placed in the mouth several times, they began to salivate when they saw the food *before* it went into the mouth. From this observation he correctly concluded that salivating to the *sight* of food was a learned reaction—a reaction that arose from the experience of pairing two events: (1) sight of food and (2) food in mouth. Later Pavlov found that dogs could easily learn to associate food-in-mouth with virtually any event which occurred with it, such as the sound of a bell or the onset of a light, and they would begin to salivate when this event occurred.

How does this relate to the way we learn fears? The dogs were learning that the bell or light was a *signal* that food would be in the mouth soon. It's as though they came to think, "Oh boy, there's the bell. I can hardly wait to taste that yummy food." When we learn a fear, we are also learning a signal—but it's a signal of possible risk, threat, or danger. Icy roads become a signal that driving is risky, especially if the person previously had an accident on icy roads. This person may be thinking, "Oh no, the roads are icy. I hope I don't have an accident. I hope I don't . . . I hope I don't . . ."

Several decades ago, two psychologists, John Watson and Rosalie Rayner, demonstrated that an eleven-month-old boy named "Little Albert" could learn to fear a gentle white rat. Albert was a stable and unemotional boy—the full description sounds like an "easy" baby—and he was not afraid of the rat before conditioning began. On the contrary, he would reach for it, touch it, and giggle when it was present. He was available for the research because his mother worked as a wet nurse (breast-feeding other women's babies) at the hospital where the study was carried out.

The fear was conditioned in Albert by presenting the white rat and then sounding a loud noise by striking a steel bar with a hammer. He reacted to this noise with distress and crying. (Recall that babies are born with a fear of loud noises.) After two such pairings in one conditioning session, he showed less attraction to the rat. A week later five more pairings of the rat with the noise were presented. After this experience, the rat now elicited distress and efforts to crawl away even though the noise was no longer sounded. At one point Albert crawled away "so rapidly that he was caught with difficulty before reaching the edge of the table."[20] Clearly the rat had become a signal for the unpleasant noise—Albert learned to fear the rat by way of *classical conditioning.* *

What happened to Little Albert now that he had been subjected to this very unpleasant experience? Actually, we don't know. Watson and Rayner had planned to remove the conditioned fear, using methods that have since been found very effective in reducing fear, but Albert and his mother left the hospital before this could be done. Although the researchers speculated that the fear might "persist indefinitely," it is more likely that it diminished over time—unless, of course, he had additional negative experiences with white furry objects.

Another thing about Little Albert's fear is that it was not confined only to the rat. It *generalized* to other things that were similar or related to the rat, such as a rabbit, a bunch of cotton, a fur coat, and a Santa Claus mask. When under stress, people do not always focus on the features that distinguish signals of real danger from irrelevant objects. Thus, the fear that Jo had of flying insects (Chapter 1) was not confined only to yellow jackets. Generalization is also shown when simply being reminded of the actual frightening situation makes the person uneasy and uncomfortable.

Many other examples of fear becoming generalized come to mind:

---

*Note that research like this would not be conducted today because ethical guidelines developed by the American Psychological Association in 1973 prohibit the use of procedures that could be harmful to the child participant.

Todd was severely burned in a fire and became afraid even of a lighted match or being near heat, such as near a hot radiator.

Kim was hit by a car, and the horn sounded just before impact. She became afraid of the loud bells at church and musical horns, such as trombones and tubas.

Enid began to choke on a fish bone. She later refused to eat boneless fish and even meats that had bones attached, such as chicken and T-bone steak.

The tendency for fears to generalize helps to explain why a child's worries seem to proliferate and why the experience that triggered the fear is sometimes difficult to pinpoint. If you were Enid's parent, would you easily realize that her aversion to T-bone steak was related to the experience of choking on a fish bone?

The likelihood that a particular experience will lead to the development of fear depends on many factors, such as the child's temperament and previous experiences. It also depends on the intensity and prominence of the conditioning events and whether the events are repeated. Let's look at how parents tried to accustom their eighteen-month-old son to sea water on a beautiful, very warm day.

> The parents carried the child out till they were waist-deep and placed him in the water, face down, with their hands below him for support. Although the boy was safe from physical harm, he wasn't convinced. As a result, he was terrified, screaming and flailing about. His skin flushed from his exhausting effort. Although the child's fright should have been obvious to the parents, they did not modify their procedure. After quite some time, the parents decided that either he or they had had enough, and took him back onto the beach.[21]

The likelihood that a fear, or at least a wariness, of sea

water would develop from this experience is pretty strong. The child was face down in the water, and there was certainly the threat involving difficult breathing and unsteady physical support. Also, the sea water was all around him: he couldn't miss seeing it or feeling it, and he heard (splashes), smelled, and even tasted it. This was an almost "perfect" method for teaching fear!

Sometimes parents are instrumental in the development of fear in their child in another way: by their frequent use of excessive forms of punishment. Children are quite reasonably frightened by intense physical pain and by some other punitive methods, such as locking them in a dark closet or telling them that they are disgusting, not loved, and will be given away. Virtually all parents use punishment at some time or other that frightens their children. The occasional use of moderate punishment probably does not lead to serious fears, but excessive punishment can.

It has become shockingly clear that there are many parents who use extreme levels of punishment that go way beyond the typical spanking. Child abuse has become a well-known and widespread problem[22]—more than half a million abuse cases occur each year in the United States. Children with long histories of physical abuse tend to be highly fearful and mistrusting of adults. When they are hospitalized, for example, they tend to

cry very little in general, but cry hopelessly under treatment and examination; do not look to parents for assurance; show no expectation of being comforted; are wary of physical contact and apprehensive when other children cry; are on the alert for danger and continue to size up the environment; and are constantly in search for something from people, as food, favors, or services. This is in contrast to the nonabused hospitalized child who clings to parents, turns to parents for assurance, demonstrates a desire to go home and is reassured by parents' visits.[23]

Probably because of the abuse these children have suffered, they see the world as a scary place where, in private, grownups inflict pain and fail to provide children with care when hurt or comfort when unhappy.

Avoidance and Reward

The child's experience provides a source of fear in two other ways: the child's *avoidance* of fearful situations and certain "side benefits" or *rewards* that being afraid may bring. Pat, the very fearful boy in Chapter 1, was afraid of many things, including taking exams and speaking before a group. When these events were scheduled, he became physically ill and was sent home from school. What effect did his being ill have? It allowed him to *avoid* these events, at least temporarily. Although students are usually required to make up missed exams, speeches may simply be cancelled.

Children in fear try to do something to prevent or reduce these unpleasant feelings, and avoidance is a very common method. Avoidance can take many different forms. Bonnie is afraid of dogs. The residents of a house along her usual walk to school acquired a new large dog that barks when people go by. Even though the dog is chained and in a fenced yard, Bonnie is frightened. At first she tried walking on the opposite side of the street, but that didn't work. The dog still barked at her. Now Bonnie will not walk on that block and she goes a couple of blocks out of her way to avoid encountering the dog.

Sometimes the avoidance method is masked by the child's claiming not to "like" the fearful situation. Joey has been ridiculed by other children and has withdrawn even from his friends. He is afraid of further ridicule, and he thinks that soon his friends will see how worthless he is. Now when his friends invite him to play, he declines, claiming that he doesn't like the game. Joey also declines party invitations, saying, "Parties aren't any fun." Similarly, Dennis is afraid of failing in school, especially in arithmetic. As a result, he stops studying math—saying, "I hate that stuff"—and when he inevitably flunks, he can say to himself and others: "I'm not stupid. I hate that stuff, and I didn't study. If I studied, I would pass. It's not really a failure if you don't try."

It is easy to see that the avoidance behavior of Joey and Dennis are counterproductive because they are not acquiring important social and academic skills. But what's the problem in Bonnie's avoidance behavior? You could argue that, "After all, walking is good exercise, and the extra walk will do her good." How is this harmful to her?

First of all, children need to come to grips with—or gain a sense of self-control over—the stresses they experience. By avoiding encounters with dogs, Bonnie is cancelling opportunities to reduce her fear and to gain control. If, instead of avoiding dogs, she allowed at least some mild and tentative encounters, she might learn that most dogs are "all bark and no bite." After a while the experiences she would have might be somewhat more bold, including petting friendly dogs, and she would learn about all the fun they can be. By this *gradual progression* in the boldness of these experiences, Bonnie's fear would be replaced by pleasant feelings.

A second problem with avoiding fearful situations is that sometimes the avoidance behavior can get worse and become more disruptive, especially if these situations are common in everyday life. There are many millions of dogs in the United States, and almost all of them live where people do, not out in the wilderness. The one dog on Bonnie's old route to school is not the only one she will have to avoid. Eventually she may refuse to go anyplace where a dog may be. This might include parks, playgrounds, beaches, shopping malls with pet stores—in effect, anywhere outside of her home. Avoidance that reaches this extent is obviously undesirable, and it is important for the child to overcome fears before they become firmly-entrenched, serious problems.

If being afraid is an unpleasant feeling, what rewards does it bring? For one thing, avoidance behaviors generally produce an immediate reduction in the child's anxiety. As Bonnie walks to school, she reaches a choice'point: "Do I go the more direct route past that nasty dog, or do I go the long way?" She feels anxious at the prospect of encountering the dog, and choosing to go the long way reduces that anxiety, at least until the next time.

But being afraid often brings many other kinds of rewards or "side benefits" that therapists call *secondary gain*. When Pat became ill at school, he not only avoided or postponed exams and speeches, but he got to stay home and do things he enjoyed, such as watching TV, reading comic books, or playing with toys. These are side benefits of becoming ill and being home from school.

Other secondary gains may also accrue. Pat might be allowed to skip his usual chores at home, and he may receive other special privileges, such as his choice of TV programs "because he's sick." He also becomes the recipient of a great deal of attention from his parents. This is not to say that parents should be unconcerned and uncaring when their child is frightened or when he is physically ill. But parents can be watchful of what is happening, and they can attempt to help the child overcome the fears that may be leading to his need for attention. If parents see signs that the child's fearfulness is increasing, they might do well to ask themselves, "What is he getting out of his fears?"

Observational Learning

Four-year-old Jackie is helping her mother clean and straighten up the basement. As her mother moves a box of junk, they see a mouse run out from behind it. Mother screams, "My God, it's a mouse," picks up Jackie, runs upstairs, and orders her daughter: "Don't go down there anymore." Children learn many things by observing other people, and Jackie learned by watching her mother that mice are things to be afraid of. During the early childhood years, children become increasingly attuned to signs of fear in other people.[24]

Being able to tell when other people are afraid is a very adaptive skill because these cues help to protect the child when real danger exists. But this ability also provides another avenue by which the child acquires new fears. The child's parents, as "models," are important in this regard. Children, especially young ones, admire and respect their parents as competent, powerful problem-solvers who protect them from danger. If children see mommy or daddy reacting fearfully toward something, they are likely to think that real danger exists. Therefore, it is not surprising that children tend to acquire their parents' phobias, particularly for dogs, insects, and storms.[25] Jackie's mother who is afraid of mice not only provided a model for fearful behavior, but in the presence of a mouse was unable to be constructive in helping to prevent fear from developing in her child.

Children also learn fears by observing phobic reactions in other children.[26] In one study, youngsters (with their parents' permission) watched a short film that portrayed a five-year-old boy screaming and withdrawing when his mother simply showed him a plastic figure of a cartoon character, Mickey Mouse; but when his mother showed him a plastic figure of Donald Duck, he responded in a calm and undistressed manner. After the children watched this film, they participated in a task that involved the Mickey Mouse and Donald Duck figures. At this time they tended to avoid the Mickey Mouse figure (the one feared by the boy) in favor of the Donald Duck. Initially this avoidance reaction was pronounced—but a day or two later, the children showed no avoidance or preference for either figure.

Observing fear in other people not only influences our outward behavior, it also produces *internal* reactions. When we experience fear, reactions occur inside our bodies: our muscles become tense, hearts beat faster, and so on. This happens also when we observe other people in fearful situations. Have you ever witnessed someone make an embarrassing blunder while making a speech? To the extent that you "put yourself in his place," you probably felt an internal reaction, such as muscle tension, and thought "Oh, that poor guy." In the study I just described, the researchers measured the internal physical reaction of children as they watched the film. The children showed greater internal reaction during the Mickey Mouse (fearful) episode than during the Donald Duck.

Although children's fears can be increased by observing almost anyone's fearful behavior, not all frightened people have the same impact as "models" of fear. The impact of other children as fearful models is greatest if they are similar to the observing child in characteristics such as age.[27] Consciously or unconsciously, the child may think: "If a child who is a lot like me is afraid, maybe I should be, too." Fearful models who are different from the child may also have a strong impact if the child perceives them as generally powerful and competent. Here, the child might think, for instance, "If that big, strong guy thinks a dog could hurt him, what could a dog do to skinny little me?"

Children watch a great deal of television—generally between 15 to 25 hours a week, and some watch three times that much.[28] Many of these children sit there almost mesmerized, observing and learning. TV provides a very powerful source for observational learning. For one thing, children see models of fearful behavior in many different situations—people who are afraid of the dark, of harmless animals, and so forth.

Perhaps more importantly, TV presents many *unrealistic and exaggerated situations that can frighten children.*

Three-year-old Freddy seemed completely delighted, curled up with his parents while watching an eerie "horror" movie on TV. It had goblins and dragons, and Freddy squealed with pleasure when they appeared. Sometimes he covered his eyes, but it was more out of excitement than fear—something like a peekaboo game. Then the very first vampire he had ever seen appeared. It looked like an ordinary person, but then it opened its mouth! Freddy seemed calm as he leaned forward and stared at the TV. But after the movie was over and he had gotten ready for bed, he began to whimper and ask to stay up for a while. Soon it became clear that he was too frightened to sleep, and his parents stayed up most of the night trying to reassure him that vampires really don't exist.

TV also exaggerates the threat of danger in *real, but highly unlikely, possible events.* The many crime programs, with gangsters, murderers, and violence, make children fearful of criminal attack. After all, TV criminals seem to be everywhere, and their frequent violence against innocent victims suggests to children that this danger is very likely and unavoidable. Furthermore, the focus on murders, robberies, and arson in the newspapers and on TV news programs confirms this exaggerated belief. This is not to say that people do not need to be cautious, particularly in high-crime areas. But some children develop phobias that relate to being attacked by criminals and then refuse to go outside, for instance.

Another exaggeration on TV occurs when animals and insects are portrayed as vicious monsters that, sometimes "conspiring" in large numbers, seek out and attack humans. Movies like *The Birds* or *The Swarm* are clear examples, but *Jaws* may have had the most widespread impact. The summer when *Jaws* was playing in theaters, a news story reported that people were staying away from beaches in droves. Not just children, but adults were afraid of being attacked, dismembered, and killed by marauding sharks. The observation of scary portrayals of animals, violence, and monsters on TV and in the movies can impair children's psychological development.

One other way that a child learns fears from other people is from the warnings and information they provide. For example, six-year-old Kathy was given so many warnings about dangers that she began to think that the world was a terrifying place. There was a whole "list" of these warnings.

"Don't go near the water, or you'll drown."
"Don't cross the street, or you'll be run over."
"Don't look like you're afraid of the dog, or he will bite you."
"Don't climb on the jungle-gym, or you'll fall."
"Don't lie, or God will send you to hell."
And so on. . . .

She was also informed that snakes are "slimy" and "poisonous" creatures that lurk in the grass, in trees, in water, and under rocks, waiting to bite her with their dreaded fangs.

In fact, Kathy had heard so many negative things and warnings about dangers that she became fearful of just about anything, especially new things that she was unfamiliar with. When she received a new toy, she would think something like "It looks like fun, but I wonder if it will pinch me." This fearful attitude can hinder her development because she is less willing to explore, be adventurous, and take the kind of reasonable risks that help children to master their fears and feel competent in having some measure of control.

Sometimes the warnings that adults give are deliberately designed to frighten the child in order to accomplish goals they think are important. A parent might warn, "If you don't eat your vegetables, I'll call the doctor and he'll give you a shot," or "Don't play near the lake because a giant octopus will jump out of the water and eat you up." Certainly it is important to set reasonable limits for children and to protect them from injury, but these goals should be achieved by helping them to understand the need for reasonable precautions rather than by terrifying them.

In summary, the many types of experiences that children have with frightening events provide an important source for the development of fear. Indeed, research identifying the things that are frightening to people has shown that these fears are determined, in large measure, by

the individual's personal and social situation; for example, the elderly fear loneliness and physical injury, students fear examinations, lower SES [socio-economic status] boys fear switch-blades and beatings, and young children, still learning the limits of reality, fear ghosts, witches, and darkness. The fears are appropriate to age, social class and role, culture, and even moment in history. Thus, the normative data suggest that what is feared by children is largely determined by social and historic fashion as well as by individual experiences.[29]

4

Thinking and Imagination as Sources of Fear

Kids Say the Darndest Things is the title of a delightful and popular book written by TV personality Art Linkletter many years ago. Children not only *say* the "darndest things," they *think* them and *imagine* them too. Sometimes children's thinking and imagination can create threats in their minds that lead to fears. Often these fears seem "silly" to adults.

RACHEL'S THINKING

Rachel, at almost three years of age, has developed a fear of taking a bath. During infancy she always enjoyed her bathinette and would playfully splash water around. The transition to bathing in the tub seemed easy for her, and she loved to play in the water with her rubber toys. Because she never had an accident in the tub, such as falling and hurting herself, Rachel's mother is puzzled by her sudden protests, crying, and tantrums at bath-time.

Although some two-year-olds may refuse baths as part of the stubbornness that parents are told to expect in the period called the "terrible twos," Rachel's resistance has a different source. She has become afraid of bathing. And this *fear arose from incorrect ideas she thought up all by herself that involved extensions of things she had seen.* How did this happen?

A couple of days before Rachel's problem showed up, she was enjoying the bath her father gave her before going to bed. She started to play with the knob that controls the drain, and flipped it to the open position. Because the bath was almost finished, her father left the drain open. As she stood up for her father to dry her off, she noticed that the water level dropped, as she had seen in previous baths when she stood up—but this time it didn't stop! It kept dropping while she stood there, and toward the end she watched carefully as the last of the water began swirling and making a strange noise as it was sucked down the drain. Suddenly Rachel grabbed onto her father, saying "Take me out, Daddy." He hadn't realized what she was thinking, and, since she was dry, he picked her up and carried her off to bed.

What was Rachel thinking as she watched the water go down the drain? Although it may seem a bit absurd, she was afraid that she would be sucked down the drain too! Where would she get such an idea? For one thing, she had seen things flushed down the toilet, never to return. "But these were small things," you note.

True enough. But Rachel did not understand yet that large, solid things don't fit in small holes. (Except, of course, if they are reshaped by extraordinary pressure, for example. But she's probably better off not being informed of that!) So, as she watched the water drain, she noticed that the original amount of bath water was "bigger than me," and *it* went down the drain. Also, on earlier occasions she had seen cartoons in which a person (actually, a genie) had emerged from, and withdrew back into, a small spout. Rachel's thinking may have been faulty, but it seemed very logical to *her*—and that's what counts. Her *thinking* provided the source of her fear.

As the Ability to Think Develops

Earlier we saw that the fears of infants and toddlers tend to involve tangible and immediate events, especially if associated with pain, loud noises, and so on. Between two and six years of age children's ability to think improves quickly, and they become able to use their memories to consider what could happen in the future, as Rachel did.

Young children also begin to think about abstract concepts and conjure up some sort of image for these things—as they might for the "Gobble-uns" in the classic children's poem *Little Orphant Annie* by James Whitcomb Riley:

You better mind yer parents, and yer
  teachers fond an' dear . . .
Er the Gobble-uns 'll get you
  Ef you
    Don't
      Watch
        Out!

In this way, children begin to fear *ideas* that they were unaware of and about which they have very little knowledge. These fears are especially likely to arise if parents and teachers use such ideas to scare children into "being good," as the poem could do.

The ability to reason—that is, to think in a logical fashion—can help an individual avoid the development of some fears. If Rachel had been able to think logically about the properties of water, the relative size of her body compared to the drain hole, and so on, she would not have been afraid of being sucked down the drain. But the ability to reason develops gradually throughout childhood and into adolescence.[30] As a result, children are often unable to use logic to defend against fears.

Some characteristics of the young child's thinking "don't make sense" to adults, but they lend a charming quality to childhood. One of these characteristics is called *animism,* and it involves the belief that inanimate objects possess life, consciousness, and will—just as people do. Until about six or seven years of age, the child might think that the sun is alive "because it gives light," or that a clock is alive "because it goes," or that an oven is alive "because it cooks my supper," or that a tree is only alive "when it has fruit on it." Anything that does something or has a use may be thought of as alive by the young child.

Jean Piaget, the well-known developmental psychologist, described these and many other examples of animism in the thinking of the children he studied.[31] For instance, one child was talking about hanging a metal box from a string. When he let go of the box, it began to turn because the string was twisted. The reasons he gave for why the twisted string began to unwind showed that he believed the string has consciousness and will: When asked why a twisted string turns, he answered, "Because it wants to unwind itself." And when asked whether a twisted string knows it is twisted, he replied "Yes . . . . Because it wants to untwist itself, it knows it's twisted . . . . Because it feels it is all twisted."

Animistic beliefs can be delightful, but they can also lead to fears. Two-year-old Nancy was already a little timid around vacuum cleaners and their loud roar. One day she thought her mother was going to do some cleaning, and she asked "Where's the BAK-OOM?" Her mother, knowing Nancy's fear of vacuums and wanting to defuse it, answered playfully, "It's OK. He went upstairs to sleep. Do you feel better now?" At first Nancy nodded that she felt better, but then she began to cry. Her mother's fanciful answer held an animistic notion that Nancy hadn't thought of yet. And if "he" could go upstairs to "sleep," couldn't he wake up and come down?

Sometimes the fear of vacuum cleaners relates to their function—sucking things from the floor—and the child may think, animistically, that vacuums "eat." Nancy became afraid that vacuums can "eat me up." This thinking is something like Rachel's fear of being sucked down the drain with her bath water.

Another characteristic of young children's thinking that Piaget called "realism" might be a little more clearly described as *over-realism*. This is when children tend to see psychological events, such as thoughts, feelings, and dreams, as real thinglike entities. The following conversation with five-year-old Barb illustrates over-realism in the child's conception of what a dream is:

Interviewer: Do you ever have dreams?
Barb: Yes, I dreamt I had a hole in my hand.
Int: Are dreams true?
Barb: No, they are pictures we see.
Int: Where do they come from?
Barb: From God.
Int: Are your eyes open or shut when you dream?
Barb: Shut.
Int: Could I see your dream?
Barb: No, you would be too far away. . . .
Int: Is the dream in the room or inside you?
Barb: It isn't in me or I shouldn't see it!
Int: And could your mother see it?

Barb: No, she isn't in the bed. Only my little sister sleeps with me.[32]

It is not until nine or ten years of age that children recognize that dreams are the products of thought, which occurs inside the head, and the eyes don't actually see a dream. The child now says "It's *as if* you could see it." Because younger children tend to believe dreams are real entities that they "see," they are more likely to believe nightmares are real and to be frightened by them.

IMAGINATION AND FANTASY

Part of the "magic" of childhood is in the imagination and fantasy of youngsters in their early years. Some of the things that children imagine, they also believe are real. Thus, over-realism and animism are features of children's imagination.

Between two and five years of age, a majority of children invent at least one *imaginary* companion or "playmate" with whom they engage in lengthy dialogues and games.[33] And since youngsters do not distinguish between real and unreal things as clearly or objectively as older children and adults do, they sometimes believe these imaginary companions are real. Not long ago, children who talked to and played with these companions were thought to be lonely, unhappy, and hallucinating—signs that reflect psychological maladjustment. Today, however, many psychologists believe that this kind of imagination, within limits, serves many useful functions as children develop.

What useful function does an imaginary companion provide? Children may sometimes rely on their invented friend when they are afraid. They might imagine that this friend can scare away monsters, or protect them during thunderstorms, or make sure they are safe at night in bed. Selma Fraiberg,[34] a well-known child psychoanalyst, described a classic example of a child who seemed to use an imaginary companion to help master fears. The child was her two-year-old niece, Jan, who was afraid of animals that could bite, such as dogs. One afternoon as Fraiberg entered the house of Jan's grandparents:

> Jan did not greet me; if anything, she looked a little annoyed at my entrance, like the actress who is interrupted during rehearsal by a clumsy stage-hand who blunders on stage. Still ignoring me, Jan pulled on her white cotton gloves and clasped her patent purse in her hand in a fine imitation of a lady leaving an afternoon engagement. Suddenly she turned and frowned at something behind her. "No!" she said firmly. "No, Laughing Tiger. You *cannot* come with us for an ice-cream cone. You stay right there. . . ."
>
> There had been a steady influx of imaginary companions in this household and an even greater number in the child's own. There were chairs which were sacred to Jane and Tommy, places reserved at the table for rabbits, dogs, and bears. . . . I noticed now that the child's grandmother looked a little distraught, and I realized that she must have had Laughing Tiger under foot for most of the afternoon.
>
> "Why *Laughing* Tiger," I asked.
>
> "He doesn't roar. He never scares children. He doesn't bite. He just laughs."
>
> "Why couldn't he go for an ice-cream cone?"
>
> "He has to learn to mind. He can't have everything his own way. . . . Anyway that's the way it was explained to me."
>
> At dinner that evening my niece did not take notice of me until I was about to sit down. "Watch out!" she cried. I rose quickly, suspecting a tack. "You were sitting on Laughing Tiger!" she said sternly. . . . "You can go now, Laughing Tiger," said Jan.

Laughing Tiger remained as Jan's imaginary companion for several months. She probably used him to give her a kind of control over her fearful feelings about animals—as Fraiberg described:

> Now if you are very little and helpless before dangers, imaginary or real, there are not too many solutions handy, good solutions anyway. You could, for example, stay close to mother or daddy at all times and let them protect you. Some children go through such clinging periods and are afraid to leave a parent's side. But that's not a good solution. Or you could avoid going outside because of the danger of an encounter with a wild beast, or you could avoid going to sleep in order not to encounter dream animals. . . . . [But these] are poor solutions . . .
>
> Now there is one place where you can meet a ferocious beast on your own terms and leave victorious. That place is in the imagination. . . . All of the dangerous attributes of tigers underwent a transformation in this new creation. Teeth? This tiger doesn't bare his teeth in a savage snarl; he laughs. . . . Scare children? *He* is the one who is scared. Wild and uncontrolled? One word from his mistress and this hulk shrinks into his corner. Ferocious appetite? Well, if he exhibits good manners, he *may* have an ice-cream cone.

When Jan's fear of animals had largely subsided, Laughing Tiger disappeared and no other imaginary animal replaced him. Fraiberg concluded that Jan had used him to help overcome her fear and work toward her own strengthened psychological development.

Is the development of children strengthened by having imaginary playmates? There is reason to believe that it is. Research has found that, compared with children who claim to have no imaginary companions, those who do have them tend to be brighter, more cooperative and less aggressive, better at concentrating and seldom bored. In addition, they watched much less TV; and when they did watch, they did not care as much for cartoons and violent shows. It may be that children who have imaginary companions can develop and practice social and language skills that might otherwise develop less quickly.

In most instances, imaginary companions in early childhood are not considered to be signs of emotional maladjustment. However, if a child has difficulty forming human ties and seems to be abandoning the real world, and if a child consistently prefers imaginary playmates over real ones, there is cause for concern. Imaginary companions tend to drop out as children grow older, and most children abandon them by around six years of age.

One problem with children's imagination, as we have seen earlier, is that it can sometimes *produce* fears rather than eliminate them. Although children usually realize that the imaginary playmate is "just make-believe"—even though they may set a place at the dinner table for him— sometimes a child may confuse imaginary and real events.[35] If the child is frightened by certain imagined events and believes they are real, a fear may develop. This was illustrated in Chapter 1 with the boy named Pat who imagined he was surrounded by "monster things" as he lay in bed. Watchful and sensitive parents, rather than leaving a child to his own devices, can keep in touch with the child's make-believe world and help to guide it in a positive direction.

Fairy tales, nursery rhymes, and story books offer children an enchanted window through which to see the world. But these fantasy experiences *can have impact on the child in both positive and negative ways*. On the positive side, child psychologist Bruno Bettelheim[36] considers fairy tales—even frightening ones—to be excellent entertainment for the child, having a predominantly beneficial effect on psychological development. He claims that fairy tales teach children not only about "correct ways of behaving," but about the good and bad realities of life:

> Many parents believe that only conscious reality or pleasant and wish-fulfilling images should be presented to the child—

that he should be exposed only to the sunny side of things. But such one-sided fare nourishes the mind only in a one-sided way, and real life is not all sunny. (p. 7)

He also points out that fairy tales teach important basic values of society, such as striving for goals, working hard, and planning and foresight:

> Fairy tales, unlike any other form of literature, direct the child to discover his identity and calling, and they also suggest what experiences are needed to develop his character further. Fairy tales intimate that a rewarding, good life is within one's reach despite adversity—but only if one does not shy away from the hazardous struggles without which one can never achieve true identity. These stories promise that if a child dares to engage in this fearsome and taxing search, benevolent powers will come to his aid, and he will succeed. . . . those who are too timorous and narrow-minded to risk themselves in finding themselves must settle down to a humdrum existence. . . . (p. 24)

> . . . . "The Three Little Pigs" teaches the nursery-age child in a most enjoyable and dramatic form that we must not be lazy and take things easy, for if we do, we may perish. Intelligent planning and foresight combined with hard labor will make us victorious over even our most ferocious enemy—the wolf! (pp. 41–42)

But what about the possible negative impact that fairy tales may have? Many psychologists and parents object to the violence, improbable events, and simplistic psychology that are woven into these stories. Concerning the fears the stories can produce, Bettelheim says, "A particular story may indeed make some children anxious, but once they become better acquainted with fairy stories, the fearsome aspects seem to disappear, while the reassuring features become ever more dominant"(p. 122).

Perhaps this is so for some children, but other kids seem to have more difficulty than Bettelheim claims. For instance, researchers have found that the fear of "monsters" (witches, goblins, etc.), animals, and insects are among the most prevalent worries of young children. And why are these fears so prevalent? Many psychologists believe these fears may be fanned by stories about the nasty kidnapping witch in *Hansel and Gretel,* the ferocious and violent wolf in *The Three Pigs,* and the fright of *Little Miss Muffet* when the spider sat down beside her.

Should parents and teachers stop telling children fairy tales and nursery rhymes? No, that would be an overreaction. Many nursery stories and rhymes help children overcome fears and promote useful values, skillful reasoning, and personality development. But adults need to be *selective* about the stories they tell. Just as many parents are screening out certain TV shows from their children, adults can *select* (or even modify) stories to match the age, fears, life situation, and personality of *each individual child.*

FEELINGS ABOUT POWER AND HELPLESSNESS

Children who feel helpless in the face of danger are vulnerable to fears. That is why one of the most important messages children can learn from their experiences, thinking, and fantasies is: "I am not helpless. I am a competent person who can achieve goals and take care of myself. I can master and control happenings in my world if I try." Children who do not get this message feel that they are incompetent and not very worthwhile individuals—their self-concepts are negative. Children with negative self-concepts tend to suffer high levels of anxiety and poor school adjustment.[37]

Young infants are very helpless creatures, but they begin to strive toward attaining control and mastery right from the start. Two-month-old Donna, lying tummy down, has to struggle to lift her head and see what's going on around her, but she does it. At five months she will struggle to roll over onto her back so she can play with her crib mobile. Later she will struggle to pull herself to a standing position, then to walk. Life has many struggles to be mastered.

Young children lack power and competence in many of the situations they encounter. Compared with adults, children are physically smaller and weaker, less experienced, and less capable intellectually. What's more, they *realize* this—perhaps never more clearly than when facing danger. This is partly why they develop so many fears in early childhood.

But as children grow, and as they gain confidence in their ability to master and control events, they begin to have faith in their own ability to take care of themselves; they believe they can cope successfully with situations that otherwise would be perceived as threatening. This is what Albert Bandura, a highly regarded researcher and theorist, calls *personal efficacy.*[38]

When life becomes difficult or stressful, children who lack a sense of personal efficacy may stop trying, thinking, "Oh, what's the use." Instead of feeling they have power and control, they feel helpless or defeated-before-the-fact. These children are afraid that their efforts will be futile and that trying will only lead to failure and embarrassment.

That is what happened with a boy named Art. When he was in first grade, he missed several weeks of school because of illness. Up to that point he had been, at best, an "average" student. So when he returned to school he had to spend a great deal of time making up the work that he couldn't do during the illness. His biggest deficiency was in reading, so he was often taken out of class to work with a specialist. Unfortunately this extra help usually pre-empted his spelling period, and he began to fall behind in this area even though his reading improved. When he did attend his spelling periods, he tried to learn but he made a lot of errors.

Art's second-grade teacher introduced spelling bees. Since he had gotten no specific help in spelling, he was always one of the first to be eliminated. In third grade, spelling contests were held in class with several "teams" competing. When the team members were chosen, no one wanted Art. He would see their faces when he was finally assigned to a team, and sometimes the team-mates would protest, or try to trade him, or say things like "Now we'll lose for sure," or "He's *Art*, not sm*ART*," or "Artie's not a smartie, Artie's not a smartie" in a singsong chant that rang in his ears. By this time no one had to tell him he was a poor speller, he *knew* he was.

In later grades he had to write assignments and compositions. It had been one thing for his classmates to say he was a poor speller, but now a teacher said so too. Art got papers returned that had many misspelled words circled, and on one paper the teacher wrote in red pencil, "You must do something about this. You're *really* a poor speller!" But the teacher didn't offer special help, and he was too anxious and ashamed to seek it himself.

Most of the mistakes he made happened because he never learned many of the rules that help us to spell difficult words: rules such as "*i* before *e*, except after *c*" and the one about when to drop the *y* to form plural nouns. Art didn't realize there were rules that helped his classmates spell better than he, so he thought he was "dumb" in comparison. He was already embarrassed to have to spell publicly, but now that his papers were coming back covered with red marks, he became ashamed and anxious about writing too.

These feelings of shame, inferiority, and anxiety have a way of producing a vicious circle that escalates the problem. Art's problem with spelling began early. The errors he made in spelling periods were discouraging, but the contests made things worse. Many times during the contests he became anxious when asked to spell words he was only *pretty* sure of—"Is it rec*ei*ve or rec*ie*ve?"—and his anxiety and feelings of incompetence made him less sure. When people are unsure, but must act, they feel a sense of helplessness and are likely just to guess. That's what Art did: "rec*ie*ve." He was not a lucky guesser. These public errors made him more anxious about spelling and more convinced that "I'm just a lousy speller."

After third grade, participation in spelling bees and contests became optional. Whenever Art had a choice, he always chose whatever was the alternative to spelling. Avoidance, as we have seen, is a common response to fear. Unfortunately, his avoidance did not allow him to come to grips with his anxiety and it precluded opportunities for his spelling to improve. As a result, his spelling skills fell farther and farther behind those of his classmates at a time when the words were getting longer and more complicated. The vicious circle was becoming firmly entrenched by now.

Art's problem got still worse when his written assignments were strongly criticized for spelling errors. Now his feelings of anxiety, inferiority, and helplessness led him to misspell some words he really knew. His spelling had become "careless and sloppy." He simply gave up and stopped trying. And this is especially serious in the vicious circle because his inability to spell was now interfering with his learning to write well.

The cycle is really snowballing now, and there's no telling how seriously it will impair Art's future. But he needs help quickly to build his confidence and teach him the skills and rules for spelling. Once the vicious circle is entrenched, it becomes increasingly difficult to correct the child's problem. Clearly Art's problem could have been "nipped in the bud" if his parents and teachers had realized what was happening.

Unconscious Thoughts and Memories

Oftentimes people are unaware of the sources of their fears. In some cases, they lack awareness because the events that produced a fear occurred in very subtle ways during their lives, and they simply didn't notice what was happening. For instance, a child may not "connect" his fear of snakes with his parents' similar fear. In other cases, people lack awareness of the sources because the traumatic events happened in infancy or early childhood. Recalling the study in which eleven-month-old "Little Albert" was conditioned to fear a white rat, it is unlikely that he would have remembered the source of this fear if it persisted years after. Children's ability to remember things they experience is not well developed in the early years, but it improves as they grow older.[39]

In still other cases, people are unaware of the sources of fear because they have purged these memories from consciousness. To cope with very uncomfortable memories that generate anxiety, we sometimes use techniques that Sigmund Freud called *defense mechanisms* as a means of protecting ourselves from these thoughts. *Repression* is one type of defense mechanism whereby we exclude threatening or uncomfortable memories from conscious awareness. As a result, we *think* we have "forgotten" these thoughts—that is, we cannot recall them—but they remain in our unconscious memory and influence our behavior.

Eight-year-old Lisa developed an intense fear of anything that related to death: hearses, cemeteries, the color black, flower arrangements, and so on. But she could not think of why she should have this fear. How did this happen? Let's look at what transpired. She was the only daughter, and her father lavished his love and attention on her. Then when she was seven, her parents began to quarrel a lot. Soon Lisa's father left, and her mother bitterly told her that the breakup was "all his fault because he took up with another woman."

This was very traumatic for Lisa. She had idolized her father, but now he was gone and it was "all his fault." As a result, she began to feel great resentment and hostility toward him. When he would come for a visit, she felt awkward and uncomfortable—so uncomfortable that she wished he would not come back anymore. She wished he would die. But wishing his death was such an awful thought to her that she repressed it, banishing it from her consciousness. Soon, anything that reminded her of death also vaguely stirred this repressed wish and she would have terrible feelings of anxiety.

Many adolescents repress their concerns and thoughts that relate to sexual matters, and this can lead to anxieties. A boy who has discovered his sexual desires for women may feel that he is not attractive enough or not physically capable of satisfying a woman. Manliness is often defined by body size and muscular strength, and sexual ability is mistakenly associated with penis size. A boy who feels inferior in these areas may feel very threatened by these thoughts and repress them. In social situations with girls, such as school dances, his feelings of inferiority and the anxiety they arouse may paralyze him, making his social overtures awkward and stilted. When his advances are rejected, he may begin to dread putting himself "on the line." He may, for instance, decide that he doesn't like dancing and begin avoiding this and other courtship activities.

The degree to which individual children are aware of their motives differs greatly from one child to another. Fortunately, many—if not most—of the fears in childhood can be related to the specific sources fairly easily. But even when the sources cannot be determined, fears can usually be reduced effectively without insight into unconscious memories.[40]

5

Why Do Fears Persist and Get Worse?

Parents and other adults have the responsibility for guiding the experiences of children so that they can grow and become mature and competent persons, physically and emotionally. Although we can take precautions to make the home, school, and play areas reasonably safe, many of the frightening and painful events in the lives of children are inevitable and beyond our control. After all, we cannot always be there to shield children from danger, or always know that they need our help, or always know what is the best thing to do.

Some of the fears children develop seem to just fade away. Others do not. What makes some fears endure, and why do they sometimes get worse?

How the Sources Perpetuate Fears

The sources of fear not only provide the roots from which fears begin, but they provide the processes by which fears are maintained. As we have seen, these sources include the child's inborn temperaments, experiences, thinking, and imagination. Let's use a hypothetical case to illustrate how these sources can maintain a child's fears, and make them worse.

Suppose a child named Alan is afraid of birds. His fear is likely to continue and get worse if:

he was born with a "difficult" temperament, making him less able to handle stressful events.

his parents are impatient, frustrated, or infuriated when he reacts fearfully to birds.

he later walks under a tree and birds swoop toward him, trying to protect their nest.

he has a painful experience or suffers an injury that he relates to birds.

he avoids birds, for instance, by staying indoors a lot.

his fearfulness leads to secondary gains, such as not having to help with outdoor chores.

his parents or friends are afraid of birds too.

he sees birds attack people on TV or in the movies.

he sees a horror movie that exaggerates the size and power of birds, for instance, an enormous bird that devours a city.

he sees a realistic film showing the predatory activities of eagles and pelicans, and then thinks that he could be the victim.

he is warned to stay away from a caged bird "because it will bite you."

he has nightmares about birds and thinks that these dreams are real events.

he has no imaginary companion to rely on for emotional protection and support.

he develops a negative self-concept and feels a sense of helplessness in stressful situations.

Any of these possibilities, and many others I didn't list, could maintain Alan's fear and make it worse. And his fear is likely to be compounded if more than one of these sources occurs. As the next section will explain, sometimes fears persist and get worse because of the way parents and other people deal with the fearful child.

THE DON'TS: METHODS THAT CAN MAKE FEARS WORSE

The mother of a nine-year-old boy once asked me, "Isn't it best that I get my fearful child into direct contact with the thing he's afraid of, even if I have to use physical force, so he will find out there's no danger?" Many parents believe this, probably as an extension of the notion that a person who falls off a horse should get right back on again.

I answered, "No. This is generally not a good idea." Forcing direct contact can be a hazardous approach. Only if he is willing, not highly fearful, and skilled in the activity, such as in riding horses, is the child likely to benefit from immediate and direct contact, assuming that danger is virtually nonexistent. In all other cases there is a substantial risk that direct contact will aggravate the fear, rather than reduce it. A few sample cases show why.

Jeff developed a fear of deep water. When he was younger, he had played in shallow pools and learned to "dog paddle." Soon after his fifth birthday, his parents took him to a lake one July where they hoped to teach him to swim. Jeff was frightened of this large body of water, and he refused to go in. After a lot of cajoling with no success, his parents carried him, kicking and screaming, into the water "for his own good." But he didn't calm down and learn that there was no danger—he flailed about, swallowed some water, began to choke, and threw up. Instead of helping Jeff to overcome his initial fear, the approach his parents used made the fear worse. And their son now resented them for putting him through this ordeal.

Four-year-old Kathy went with her family to visit some relatives in the country where there were some pet geese. Everyone was saying, "Oh, aren't the geese adorable," but Kathy didn't like their honking noises and was afraid these large birds would bite her. When her aunt said, "Come here and say hello to Gary and Gilda Goose," Kathy backed away toward her mother and replied, "I don't like them." Her mother picked her up saying, "You'll like them when you feel how soft they are," carried her to Gary Goose, and put her resisting hand on his back. Kathy's eyes were closed, and she clutched her mother with her free arm as her other hand touched the feathers. She shuddered, thinking that it felt "icky," and began to whimper. That night she had a nightmare about birds chasing her.

Steve was seven years old when he began to imagine there were monsters in the dark that would kill him. One night he screamed for his parents and they came running. But when he told them his fear, his father said "That's silly; there aren't any monsters. I don't want you acting like a sissy. Now I'm going to turn off the light and close the door, and you'll see that there aren't any monsters." For many nights thereafter Steve would lie in bed trembling, sometimes silently crying himself to sleep.

From these cases you can see that direct contact with the frightening situation can make the child's fear worse, even when there is no real danger. If the child is very frightened and unwilling to participate, the positive aspects of the experience are likely to go unnoticed. When Jeff was placed in the water, he was so panicked that he didn't notice how cool and refreshing the water was. And when Kathy's hand touched the goose, her eyes were closed and she had already made up her mind that the feathers would feel "icky"—and so they did. In Steve's case, leaving him to find out there are no monsters in the darkness of his room is no help. These are creatures in his mind, not in his room. This approach simply allows his imagination to run wild.

Other methods that parents sometimes try can also aggravate the child's fears. We will look at four of these.

Ridicule and Shaming

Many children's fears seem silly to adults. We know that there are no ghosts, that a household vacuum cleaner cannot swallow a person, and that sharks are rarely near the beaches where we swim. But children—and even some adults—don't know these things, and their fears are very real to them. As a result, laughing at the fear and ridiculing it (''Now that's silly, Eddie, it won't hurt you'') *or* the child (''Don't be such a baby'') will not help. Ridicule simply makes the child feel worthless and incapable of coming to grips with fear.

A similar approach that parents sometimes try is shaming the child, especially in comparison with other children: ''There's nothing to be afraid of, Joey. Buddy isn't afraid to play with the nice doggie, are you, Buddy? Why can't *you* be a big boy too?'' This approach not only ridicules Joey's fear, but it demeans and embarrasses him in front of his friend.

It is very important for parents to take their child's fear seriously, even though it is out of proportion to the actual danger and the cause of the fear may seem silly. You don't need to pretend that the fear is real for you, but you should try to understand it and accept it as real for the child. If you do, the reassurance you give and the example you set by your own lack of fear in that situation will help the child to deal with the fear more effectively.

Scolding and Punishment

Wally's parents saw their son's fears as a sign of immaturity and as an annoyance, and they dealt with his fear reactions as "misbehaviors." When he showed fear, his parents usually scolded or punished him. They would say to him "Stop your crying—there's nothing to be afraid of. You're such a bad boy. If you don't act like a big boy soon, we're going to give you away to the mailman." Scolding and threatening the child for his fears only made Wally more fearful, and now he could add another worry to his collection: fear of separation or abandonment if his parents give him away. This was unfair to him and terribly frightening.

Punishment for expressing fears doesn't help in reducing them. It puts the child in a no-win situation. Both the feared situation and the punishment are unpleasant, and the child will do what he or she can to avoid both in the future. Ten-year-old Cheryl's school phobia met with punishment: when she cried and begged to remain home in the morning, she was spanked and sent off to school. She managed to avoid both school and punishment for quite a while by playing hooky and developing an ingenious system of lies to account for her whereabouts.

Overprotection

Another way that some parents react to fearfulness in their child is to become overprotective. From the day Sandra was born, her mother worried endlessly about her daughter's happiness and survival. Mother stayed very close to Sandra throughout the preschool years to make sure that her baby didn't injure herself. When Sandra began to walk, Mother hovered over her lest she fall down; if she climbed a chair, Mother always took her down; when she wanted to go outside, Mother always overdressed her for warmth and for padding in case she should fall. By the time Sandra was three, she was clearly a highly fearful child. Of course, her mother noticed this, and responded by redoubling her efforts to shield her daughter from all danger and all worries.

Certainly parents should take reasonable measures to protect their child, but Sandra's mother had gone much too far. As a result, her child had little opportunity to explore, build skills, and learn to cope with threatening experiences. Instead, Sandra learned that she was powerless, incompetent, clumsy, and not very bright. She lacked a sense of personal efficacy—the confidence that she is able to control events, take care of herself, and deal effectively with threatening situations. Each time she faced a difficulty, her mother stepped in and Sandra's personal efficacy suffered another setback. And each time this happened, she became more dependent on her mother.

Ignoring the Child's Fears

Some parents ignore the fear, pretending that it doesn't exist, or hoping that "it's just a phase" the child will "outgrow," or thinking that calling attention to it will embarrass the child. Ignoring the fear would be like ignoring a child's 102-degree fever—in both cases the child has a problem that *could* go away without special care, but there is a substantial risk that it could get worse instead. At the very least, action by the parents could reduce the severity and duration of the child's discomfort.

Although these approaches are common in parenting efforts, they are not constructive for helping children cope with their fears. Children whose parents use these approaches are likely to see their initial fears get worse, develop new worries caused by these methods, and become resentful of and less willing to communicate with their parents.

WHAT IF YOU DO NOTHING?

Some parents think that doing something about children's fears "puts the wrong ideas in their heads." These parents say, "By asking children if they're afraid and telling them it's all right to be afraid, you're encouraging them to be fearful. Then they become preoccupied with worries they wouldn't otherwise think about."

This belief probably has some truth to it under two circumstances. The first one I call the "out-of-the-blue" circumstance, and it exists when there is no reason to suspect that a fear might develop. The child shows no sign of fear and has never shown a related fear. For example, suppose Ricky enjoys—with reasonable caution—climbing jungle gyms and trees, and has never shown much fear of heights. When walking contentedly with his parents across a bridge one day, his father asks, "Are you afraid you'll fall off the bridge and drown in the deep river, Ricky?" Few parents would do this. It is out-of-the-blue, and it might very well plant the seed for Ricky to develop a fear of heights. Note also that this is very different from the case of little Jimmy in the dentist's office that we saw earlier. He showed signs of apprehension, and his mother used good judgment in discussing it with him.

Overprotective parents provide the second circumstance in which talking to children about possible worries may encourage them to be fearful. These parents are excessively anxious about the well-being of their children. When Brian's overprotective parents discuss his fears with him, they tend to give the impression that he *should* be afraid. Sometimes they may actually *want* the child to be fearful, thinking that if he is very frightened he will either be careful or avoid the danger entirely. But Brian will probably develop many unnecessary fears, and some may become strong enough to be "problems" because they interfere with his physical, social, or intellectual growth.

Obviously, good judgment in deciding when to take action and what to do taps your common sense, knowledge of the child, and sensitivity to his or her feelings and needs. Occasionally doing nothing about a fear may be recommended if it is *mild, uncommon,* such as of plants, and you can *keep track* of whether it is getting worse. Common fears, such as of darkness or animals, should be dealt with as soon as they appear.

Will Betty Outgrow Her Fears?

A father told me, "My daughter, Betty, is six, and she seems to be frightened of so many things—trains, cats, crippled people, darkness—lots of things. Everybody says that I needn't be concerned about her fears and she'll outgrow them in a year or so. Will she?"

The answer to this father's question is not simple. A lot depends on Betty and on her past and future experiences. What sort of temperament was she born with—was she a difficult baby or an easy one? How intense are these fears? How do her parents react to them? Does she avoid contact with fearful situations, and when she does, are there "secondary gains?" Do her parents share any of these fears? Does she feel generally powerless and incapable? Clearly, a great deal of information is needed to make any sort of prediction for a particular child, and it will not be highly accurate even then.

But I *can* describe what psychological research tells us—in an overall sense—about how long-lasting childhood fears tend to be.[41] Virtually all children overcome at least some of their fears over time, especially after a period of 2 or more years, and improvement often occurs without therapy even for some severe phobias. But the child's age and the type of fear make a difference.

Most of the fears of school-age children tend to persist for a year or longer. In contrast, preschool-age children seem to outgrow most of their fears relatively quickly, in a matter of several weeks or months. Moreover, some fears are more long-lasting than others. Although worry over physical injury often continues into adulthood and old age, fear of storms and darkness tends to decline during late childhood. Similarly, fear of animals tends to be more long-lasting than fear of strangers.

What this means is that Betty's father—and you—should not assume that a child's fears are likely to be outgrown. Even if a fear does decline, the process and discomfort will probably go on for several months or years. And don't forget, some fears get worse.

Dollars and Sense

I have a great investment for you, and there's very little risk. You'll need to put up a modest deposit of effort and sensitivity, and you can save a great deal of discomfort, annoyance, time, and money.

Professional therapy for a child's serious fears can be very costly. Depending on the severity of the problem and the type of therapy used, the bill could come to as little as 200 dollars, or as much as a few thousand. It also takes time and money to find a good therapist and to go in for office visits. Wouldn't you rather use your time and money for other necessities?

As important as time and money are, the major concern of most parents is with the difficulties fearful children experience and the strains imposed on the parent-child relationship. As children grow older, their problems with fear can cause increasing difficulty for them. They are expected to develop socially, and their age-mates will want them to join in many new activities that may be frightening. Those who cannot join in these adventures suffer a disadvantage in making friends. And their fears can become a source of embarrassment to themselves and their parents.

Embarrassment over the child's fears was one of the causes for problems in the parent-child relationship of a ten-year-old boy named Pat. This is the boy I described at the beginning of the book who was terrified of the dark, shy, highly self-conscious, and constantly worried about his schoolwork. Because fear of the dark is unusual in a boy his age, he and his parents were embarrassed when people found out. For instance, his family stayed over night at the home of relatives, and Pat bunked-in with his cousin. As he prepared for bed, Pat called his mother aside and asked if she had brought the night light, but she hadn't. When he began to fuss, she said sternly, "Look. I forgot the light, and I'm sorry. Aunt Jane doesn't have one, so I want you to try very hard to do without it. It's just for one night."

Pat did try very hard, but he couldn't control his fear. He had hoped, at least, that his cousin would go to sleep quickly so that his terror wouldn't have an audience. But his cousin was so excited at having a guest that he talked and talked. All the while, Pat didn't listen to a word—he only heard the popping, pounding, snapping, and gurgling noises of this strange house. "The monsters are here, and they're noiser than ever!" he kept thinking.

Suddenly Pat shrieked and trembled uncontrollably. He had held it in as long as he could, but he just couldn't any longer. His cousin was so shocked by this spectacle that he ran for help, which was already on the way. The whole house had heard the shrieking. As everyone hovered over him, Aunt Jane kept saying, "I never realized it was this bad."

Pat finally went to sleep on a cot close to his parents. The next day he didn't want to face anyone, and his relationship with his parents was impaired for several days by their mutual embarrassment, frustration, desperation, and anger. "What are we going to do about Pat?" he overheard his father say. And his mother answered, "I'm at my wits' end. We've tried everything."

Pat's parents *thought* they had "tried everything," but

they really hadn't. They were unaware of the many techniques that can effectively help children overcome fears, and they should have begun using them years ago.

How can you help children cope? The remainder of the book tells you how.

6

Helping Before the Fear Is Strong

The mother of Jimmy who was afraid at his first visit to the dentist was sensitive to his wariness, so she calmly and honestly explained what would happen during the examination. By doing this she could help *prevent* a strong fear from developing. Prevention is the first line of defense in helping the child cope with fear.

This chapter describes techniques that are appropriate before the fear is strong. Chapter 7 suggests methods to be tried with stronger, more persistent fears. Depending on the circumstances, you may find it reasonable to juggle some techniques around somewhat. So much depends on the individual child, what the fear is, and why he or she is afraid of it. In Chapter 8 I'll describe methods that help in preventing, nipping, and reducing each of fifteen common childhood fears.

AN OUNCE OF PREVENTION

To some extent we can ''immunize'' children against many of the fears of childhood by helping each child develop a strong self-concept. *Children who have confidence in their ability to master and control events and challenges in their lives are less vulnerable to fear.* In contrast, children who think negatively about their power and ability tend to perceive people, animals, and situations as more powerful and potentially threatening.

How can you help a child to develop a healthy confidence in his or her abilities? You can begin right from birth. One obvious but still essential way parents can enhance the child's confidence is with the kind of love that says to the baby, "We love you and respect you," "You are a worthwhile person," and "We are available and happy to guide you, protect you, take care of your basic needs, and help you to grow." These are crucial messages in building self-confidence.

How do you communicate these messages to a baby? You do it largely through touch, your eyes and facial expression, and tone of voice. You say to the baby "I love you" by giving tender caresses, affectionate stroking, and secure holding; looking the baby in the eye and smiling; and using a voice that is gentle, soothing, and full of joy. Although parents can't always convey these qualities, especially when they are feeling tired or frustrated, those who use this style most of the time will get the message across.

Parents can also provide a stimulating environment in which the baby can begin to explore and test things out. After about 2 months of age babies begin to enjoy and learn important relationships from simple toys, such as crib devices that are brightly colored, movable, durable, and reachable. This early in life, babies are learning how to use their movements and senses to "make things happen." Little Lori, lying in her crib, turns her head, looks up at a hanging rattle, extends her arm, and hits it. It swings and jingles. Lori gives a crow of elation. She made it happen! This is an important beginning to believing that "I can master and control happenings in my world if I try."

Lori is fortunate because her environment continues to be stimulating and challenging as she grows. After about six months she has such appealing but simple toys as stuffed animals, stacking objects, and balls of various sizes and shapes. She picks up a ball with two pudgy little hands and shoots it (like a basketball), only it doesn't go very far. But it bounces, and she's pleased. And now she can crawl over and get it and try to throw it even farther.

She also has relatively free access to a lot of the living area, instead of being imprisoned most of each waking day in her crib and playpen. Being able to roam allows her to learn many new things, such as what doors do and how to open and close them. Certainly by nine months of age, infants start to "get into everything," but dangerous and breakable things can be put out of reach. Lori's access to the living area also allows her to find her parents when she is feeling lonely or frightened. Now she doesn't have to make a big fuss so they will come to her; she can go to them and feel protected simply by making sure they are nearby.

Lori's parents do something else that helps her learn new skills and develop confidence in her own abilities to cope with her world. They encourage her to try new and appropriate activities by *guiding* her actions and *praising* her accomplishments, even the ones that seem simple to adults. For example, when Lori was physically ready to climb steps, her parents showed her how, helped her to balance, and told her what a good job she was doing.

Some parents would have short-circuited this and other opportunities for Lori to gain confidence in herself. They would take over for the child. If they approached some stairs, they would pick her up because they are impatient with her slow climbing, or overprotective, thinking that she'll fall and hurt herself. These parents also tend to verbalize their reasons, saying "I can't wait all day" or "Here. I'll carry you so you won't fall." Not only does this child miss out on opportunities to develop skills early, but this kind of parenting leads her to doubt her power and ability to take care of herself, rather than having faith in herself.

Other parents would take a completely opposite approach, but have a similarly negative effect on the child. These parents set excessively high standards and *expect* the child to attain them. The child must mature and reach all of the developmental milestones early—walking, talking, toileting, and weaning. As the child grows older, she must be obedient, seen and not heard, a straight-A student, a winning competitor in sports or other activity, sociable, poised, and attractive. Any failure to reach these standards is a defeat for the parents.

Who can live up to these expectations? The child is doomed to anxiety and frustration, desperately trying to reach unattainable goals in an effort to please her parents. Even though she succeeds in comparison to most other children, she is devastated when she is not "the best." And no matter how well she does today, she worries that she won't meet her parents' standards tomorrow.

Lori's parents are somewhere in between these extremes. They provide opportunities and encouragement for her to attain reasonable goals. The challenges they guide her toward allow her to stretch her capacities and expand her skills. This gives her a feeling of accomplishment and success, and she can tackle new activities without constantly feeling threatened. She knows that they have confidence in her, and that they will love and accept her because she *tries her best,* not because she is *the* best. And the self-confidence her parents help her to gain will build her resistance to fear.

There are other things you can do to help prevent many childhood fears from developing. Among the most important is for you to know which fears children are most likely to develop at different ages, and then to watch for and defuse the circumstances that can frighten the child. In Chapter 2 I described the prominent sources of fear at different ages:

Infancy and Toddlerhood—strangers, separation, loud noises, bright lights, loss of physical support.

Preschool and Early School—animals and insects, dark, death (as separation, injury), doctors and dentists, heights, monsters and imaginary creatures, nightmares, school (as separation, sometimes teachers or classmates), storms and natural disasters, deep water.

Middle Childhood to Adolescence—physical injury, social relationships, inferiority, school.

If you anticipate a potentially stressful circumstance, you can defuse it by informing children in advance of the forthcoming experience, telling them what to expect, and teaching them what to do when it occurs.

Joey was four years old when he developed a medical problem: his navel began to protrude because of an umbilical hernia. His pediatrician recommended surgical repair and scheduled the operation. His parents had 2 days to try and defuse the fears that Joey might develop relating mostly to separation and bodily injury. The first thing they did was to arrange their work schedules so that at least one of them would be with him in the hospital almost constantly, day or night. Then they took the following steps. The parents

1. sat down with Joey and told him that he would have to go to the hospital so that the doctors could "fix his belly-button," which he could clearly see was puffed out. They told him he would be staying overnight, but that Mommy or Daddy would be with him most of the time. They also encouraged him to ask any questions "whenever you think of them," and answered them carefully and in a way he could understand.
2. maintained a calm and confident manner to let him know that he doesn't need to be very frightened.
3. took him to visit the hospital ward where he would be staying. They also explained the routine of hospital

life—that the nurse would wake him in the morning, how his meals will be served on a tray in bed, what to do about "going to the bathroom," that there will be other children to keep him company, and so on.

4. got a children's book from the public library that describes a boy's hospital experience, the facilities, and procedures: anesthesia, the operating room, injections, playing with other children. A book called *Curious George Goes to the Hospital* by Rey and Rey is recommended, and some hospitals have booklets, films, and other materials that can be of help.

5. both went with him when he was admitted. He brought his favorite toys and the teddy bear he always cuddles at bedtime.

6. had a nurse give an overview of some procedures he would experience on the day of the operation, including where things would happen, what he needs to do to help it go smoothly, and how the anesthetic will be given. The parents also arranged for the services of an anesthetist who is especially good in working with children and calming their fears.

7. made sure they were with him when they said they would be, especially just before the operation and when he woke up. If they had to leave him alone, they told him where they would be and when they would return.

Preventing fears that can result from hospitalization is more involved than preventing most other childhood fears, but doing so is extremely important. Pediatricians have noted that hospitalization can be so frightening that the child's physical recovery is slowed.

For older children, separation is usually less of a problem, and their primary concerns center around physical injury and death. Of course, for children of all ages who must undergo hospitalization in an emergency, without warning, you should do as much as possible to reduce traumas and make their stay minimally uncomfortable. A child who does develop fears can be helped to overcome them using the methods described later in this chapter.

Young children sometimes develop worries about bodily injury when they discover the genital differences between boys and girls. A mother described this example: Her three-year-old son, Philip, had never seen a naked girl until a five-year-old neighbor girl, Peggy, invited him to play "I'll-show-you-mine-if-you-show-me-yours." That night he awoke screaming from a nightmare, and he explained to his concerned parents that "I dreamed my wee-wee broke like Peggy's did." With further questioning, Philip described his adventure of that day and that he assumed her wee-wee had been injured.

Philip was lucky that his fear came to his parents' attention in time for them to nip it in the bud. But prevention would have been even better. Young children are very curious about differences between boys and girls. At the very least, they wonder why there are two kinds of people. Once again, information can defuse potential problems. Even at three years of age Philip understood his mother's explanation: "Boys and girls are supposed to have different bodies; they start out that way even before they are born. You were going to be a boy even before you were born. Your body is smaller than Daddy's, but you both have a wee-wee like yours. Because your body is like that, you will grow up to be a man, and you can become a daddy. Peggy's body is like mine. Because she has a girl's wee-wee— not a boy's—she can become a mommy when she grows up. It's good that you know that boys are made one way and girls are made a different way. If sometimes you don't understand things about boys and girls, we can talk about it. OK?"

Similar preventive approaches are useful in helping to

defuse potential fears in older children as they begin to mature sexually at puberty. Boys and girls can't help but notice the changes in their bodies and compare themselves with age-mates. They begin to worry about the sizes, shapes, and timing of their growth, especially if it is slower than their friends.' Susan worries, "How come my breasts haven't started to grow yet. I'll probably be flat-chested." And Bob checks every morning to see if his peach fuzz has been miraculously transformed into a beard, one of the more obvious signals of manhood, and worries that "It may never happen." As children near puberty, they need information about what to expect and how to cope with these changes and their speed. The child's same-sex parent is probably better equipped to give information and reassurance, and to share the concerns he or she had at the same age.

One of the most frightening events related to sexual maturation that an uninformed girl can have is her first menstruation. Blood flow is usually a signal of physical injury, a common source of fear at this age. If she doesn't know in advance this will happen and is too ashamed to tell anyone when it does, she may believe that she is seriously ill—perhaps dying from "internal injuries." This can be prevented if girls are informed in advance about what to expect, when it is likely to begin, and what to do when it does. They should also be told why menstruation occurs and the side-effects some women experience. Notions that many people have that women are "unclean" during menstruation should be described and dismissed. There are several books for nine- to twelve-year-olds that deal with this topic very well. One is called *The Long Secret* by L. Fitzhugh, and it deals candidly with myths that people have about "that time of the month."

Another type of fear that you can defuse by preventive methods is of monsters or imaginary creatures. What can you do? First, you know that preschool- and early-school-age children are especially prone to fears of this type. Second, you know where children find out about monsters: TV, movies, story books and comics, and stories they are told by adults and children. The best way to prevent these fears is to *watch for and restrict or modify these experiences* during the early childhood years.

Diane's parents realized that they could not see and hear every scary story or program their very young daughter would experience, but they knew they could monitor most. For instance, they began setting limits on the TV when she first started watching. When she got older, they negotiated with her the hours and shows that she could watch without asking. All other shows, movies, and story books the parents selected carefully. They kept track of movies by reading reviews and talking to peole who had seen them to find out whether anything frightening was portrayed. Her parents also made sure she had alternative activities when TV was prohibited.

All of the occult and horror movies were off limits, but the parents did pick out one movie with ghosts and witches to show her. They previewed it on videotape first and decided that Diane probably wouldn't like it very much. Then they sat down with her one day and told her about the movie they would see together before supper on TV, telling her the basic plot, that "It has a lot of make-believe things in it," and they described what the ghosts and witches would look like and do.

As her parents set up the videotape, they told her, "Some people like make-believe movies, but other people don't. Let's see how we like this movie." During the film, her parents encouraged her to talk about what she felt and thought. They also played a game, "Pick out the make-believe and silly things," and at each frightening sequence involving a monster, the parents said "Oh, that's too silly. That's not fun to watch."

At the dinner table Diane's parents asked her how she

liked the movie. She replied "It was OK, but it had too much of that silly stuff." Her parents echoed her opinion and then asked her "What did you think of those ghosts and witches and the things they did?" just to make sure no fears were brewing.

Loud noises sometimes cause fears in infants and toddlers, and appliances are often the source. Preventing this fear can be accomplished by introducing the noise, especially a new noise, *gradually*. For instance, you could run a blender in the kitchen while the baby is in another room. Then with the machine still running, bring the baby to the kitchen and watch for signs of apprehension. A child who is calm and unconcerned may remain in the room in an area some distance from the blender as it runs. A child who seems frightened should be removed from the room, comforted and soothed if necessary, and introduced to it more gradually.

Also, because the child can be very startled when a loud noise comes on, suddenly breaking the relative silence, you should try to be sure the child is not nearby and other noises are already present, such as music on the radio, when you turn on the vacuum.

Most of the examples I have described for preventing fears reveal that the way children are *introduced* to potentially stressful situations is of great importance. If you recognize that a particular experience the child is about to have could lead to fear, *introduce the experience gradually*. It provides the child with less of a "shock" and more time to adapt to the experience, and it gives you the time to watch how the child is reacting.

But another important aspect of how you introduce a potentially stressful situation is the way *you* feel about it and behave. We have seen that children tend to develop fears that their parents have. Fear is contagious—the way other people react to the situation will affect the child's reaction. If you are fearful of heights, for instance, you'll probably set an example of fearfulness, rather than confidence, if you take the child on carnival rides, sight-seeing on tall buildings, or hiking near cliffs.

Parents who know they are frightened of certain situations would do well to let other adults introduce their child to those experiences. If you're afraid of deep water, enroll your child as early as possible in a swimming program so that expert instructors can introduce the joys and skills of water activities. Better still, do something to reduce your own fear—you can either get professional therapy or try to conquer it yourself with the help of a book that describes self-help methods for adults: for example, *Stop Running Scared!* by Fensterheim and Baer or *Don't Be Afraid* by Rosen.

Children don't have to acquire as many fears as they do, and developing intense, irrational fears—phobias—is psychologically counterproductive. The methods I have described in this section can help to prevent fear. The help they enable parents, teachers, and other adults to give is important for all children, especially those who are vulnerable to the development of fears. Children with "difficult" temperaments need more attention to the prevention of fear than children with "easy" temperaments.

Now that we have considered prevention, the first line of defense, we move on to the second line of defense that can be applied before a fear becomes strong. Although your use of the "first line" will not eliminate all childhood fears, fewer will need defense at the second line if you use the methods of prevention vigilantly.

Nipping Fears in the Bud

When a fear begins to develop, either because preventive measures were not taken or because it "slipped through'' the first line of defense, it should be nipped in the bud. Rather than letting the child outgrow the fear, with the risk that it will become worse, you can try to stop it dead-in-its-tracks.

In the case of Art, the boy in Chapter 4 who had problems with spelling, we saw an example of a fear that could have been stopped early. Art's problems began after he missed several weeks of school because of illness, and they became worse with repeated failures and embarrassment in spelling bees and contests. He received special help with reading, but this was at the expense of his spelling lessons where he would have learned many of the basic rules. If his teachers or parents had realized what was happening, they could have provided the tutoring he needed to improve his spelling. Whenever possible (and affordable) an extensive tutoring effort should be carried out by someone who is experienced and knowledgeable in the teacher's methods and curriculum.

Many of the fears that begin in childhood get worse because the child lacks the relevant skills needed to deal with the situation. Mary was a little frightened of dogs when her parents brought home Fritz, a friendly dachshund, but she was also self-confident and inquisitive enough to find out what he was like. Unfortunately, she didn't know how to pet and handle dogs, and she was especially attracted to his tail and floppy ears. At first he was only a little irritated by her actions, but when Mary unintentionally pinched his ear, Fritz squealed and snapped at her. This made her more frightened than she already was.

Children generally know when they lack the skills to deal with a situation effectively, and this is partly why they may be timid in their initial encounters. *Teaching relevant skills* can therefore be a very useful method for curtailing fears as soon as you notice that a child is fearful. In Mary's case, her parents could show her how to approach and play with dogs. They can also tell her what *not* to do because sometimes it can hurt the dog and they can explain that "Fritz doesn't like to be hurt, just like you don't. So he got scared. He didn't mean to hurt *you*, either. But he'll forget about it if you're good to him from now on. Let Mommy or Daddy know when you want to start playing with him and we'll help you. OK?"

Becoming accustomed to going into deep water is another situation where teaching relevant skills can be important. Most children who are afraid of water don't know how to swim. Early training in swimming skills, especially by an experienced instructor, can usually eliminate the child's mild fearfulness very quickly. If you are going to do this yourself, be sure the child:

is shown what movements are involved.

imitates those movements out of the water, on a bench or chair, for instance.

knows how to float "in case you get tired."

knows how to breathe properly in water, and what to do about breathing and swallowing problems.

initially tries shallow water, when he or she is reasonably calm, while you give lots of encouragement and physical support.

is allowed to become increasingly independent in deeper and deeper water at his or her own pace.

Also, be sure you are a friendly teacher who gives lots of careful instruction and praise, not one who becomes tense, irritable, and belittling. Take your time; don't rush.

I cannot overemphasize the importance of maintaining *open communication* with the child if you want to stop fears early. Often when children do not express their worries, their parents assume those fears don't exist. Many children hide their fears to avoid being ridiculed and called "a baby," and they feel a sense of shame in their inability to cope. Other children simply feel their parents "won't understand.'' For example, Art told his parents "I'm not good in spelling,'' and they tried to reassure him by saying "Sure you are. Spelling is easy.'' End of discussion.

Art didn't need reassurance, especially since he was right—he wasn't good at spelling. Instead, he needed to feel that he was listened to and understood and that his parents would join with him to solve his problem. How could they have handled this situation so that open communication would occur? Some "ice-breakers" might be:

"Spelling is not an easy subject, is it?"
"Some words are really tricky, aren't they?"
"It must be hard for you when you're in spelling class."
"You must be worried about what people think of you when you have trouble spelling."

These are the kinds of statements that the well-known parenting expert, Dr. Haim Ginott, recommended in his book *Between Parent and Child*. These statements say to the child "I'm listening. I understand. Let's talk about it and see if we can remedy the problem." When communication is open, you can find out how serious the child thinks the problem is.

Children need to know that being afraid is a normal feeling that all people have from time to time. This helps the communication flow, and lets the child know it's okay to talk about fears. Three methods can be very useful in helping this process along. First, you can tell the child about your own experiences with fear, especially if you had a similar fear, and you can describe how you managed to overcome it. If the fear simply disappeared as you got older, say so. At least the child will see that fear doesn't have to last forever.

A second method you can use to improve communication is to answer, and sometimes initiate, "What if. . . ?" questions, particularly with children in the four-to-six age range.[42] Children this age often ask questions that reflect their fears, such as "What if the storm made the house blow away?" or "What if I went high up the tree and I couldn't get down?" or "What if I went to school and you forgot where it was and couldn't find me?"

How should you handle "What if. . . ?" questions? Suppose Katie asked about a tornado blowing the house away. Here are some tips for her parents:

Take the time to discuss the question in a quiet and non-distracting place, either right away or sometime soon.

Answer the question honestly and give her useful information. Katie's parents could say: "We get some strong tornadoes around here, but we have a very strong house. So, it probably won't blow away. But if we get a really, really strong tornado, we will know it because the TV will tell us and we can see it coming. We won't get hurt because we will all go down into the shelter where it's safe. If the house blows away we would probably live with Grandma for a while until we can get another house."

Give straightforward answers in a calm and reasonably fearless tone.

Don't simply say that it can't happen; she thinks it can, even if it is objectively very unlikely.

Try to find out what *she thinks* will happen. This would help to pinpoint the information she needs.

Even when Katie doesn't ask, but she shows other signs of fear, *you* could *initiate* a "What if. . . ?" question: "What do you think would happen if the tornado came here?"

The third method you can use to encourage communication about fear is an intriguing one from another culture. In Malaysia, Senoi people practice dream analysis at breakfast with their children.[43] For example, suppose a boy described an anxious or frightening dream, such as one about falling. The adults would try to reshape or reinterpret the dream into one of mastery, rather than helplessness. The dialogue following the child's description might be:

Adult: That's a wonderful dream! It's one of the best dreams people can have.
Child: It wasn't so nice, to me. I was afraid.
Adult: Yes, some people get frightened when they dream they are falling. But we will try to help you understand why this dream really shows you that you are strong. When you understand that, you will think this dream is wonderful. Now, where did you fall to, and what did you discover?
Child: I didn't fall to anyplace. I was very scared, and I woke up before I got there.
Adult: Oh, that's a mistake. You must relax and enjoy yourself, and let the fall go all the way to the end. Everything that happens in a dream is important, but you won't understand it while you're asleep. A falling dream gives you one of the quickest ways to make use of the great powers of the spirit world. Soon when you have a wonderful falling dream again, you will remember that you can't really be hurt when the fall ends. Falling just takes you to the source of the power that makes the fall happen. And when you get there, you will be able to use the power so you can dream about flying, like a bird! That's why a falling dream is so wonderful.

Through discussions like this one, the Senoi try to teach the child that frightening dreams happen so he can master the problem and take control. They believe the dreamer is always in control of the dream, and that it is his own property. The frightening images the child creates are only considered negative if he or she gives up control and retreats. Therefore, they teach the child always to advance or attack when danger is in a dream, and they might tell him or her how to attack or scare the "bad" or "evil" image.

These images will only continue to seem frightening if the child refuses to come to grips with them.

We have seen that a frequent source of children's fears is their imagination, and this is fed by the stories they see and hear from TV and movies. Parents and other adults can help children draw a clear line between make-believe and reality.

When children talk about witches, goblins, cartoon animals, or other characters they have heard about, you can pleasantly engage in dialogue that reminds them that these characters are make-believe. This is especially effective if you can guide children to their own statements or conclusions that the characters are not real. Most importantly, don't ridicule their talking about make-believe things or dismiss their stories out-of-hand. This only stops communication.

Often children who hear a story will ask, "Is it true, or is it make-believe?" Sometimes they are asking exactly that but at other times they are covertly asking, "Is this something that could actually happen to *me? Am I safe?*" These children need to know that these events cannot take place in reality or in the here and now, but only in the never-never land of make-believe. Therefore the witches in the stories can never hurt real people—they can only hurt make-believe people.

Children's thinking often leads to fears because of misunderstandings. For instance, Kim refused to go down into Grandpa's cellar because "the scary monster with all those arms" would get her. Actually, Kim's monster was the furnace with ducts and pipes extending from it, and it made ominous noises when it kicked on. To make things worse, she once asked what that noise was and was told, "Oh, the furnace is running." "Running!" she thought, envisioning this monster scurrying around like an octopus.

In this kind of situation, a straightforward *explanation* can nip the fear in the bud. Her parents realized what was happening, and they took the time to go with Kim and look at her monster. They explained what the furnace does to keep them warm in winter, why the ducts and pipes were needed, and that the word "running" does not always mean "moving around," but can mean "working or operating." After this explanation, she quickly lost her fear.

Sometimes *helping the child feel in control* of the feared object can eliminate the fear. Kim's parents also showed her how the thermostat works and let her turn the furnace on and off a few times, making it into a game where they would run over to a heating duct and wait for hot air to emerge. In a similar vein, a friend/colleague told me about a fear her daughter Sarah had once had of vacuum cleaners. The fear went away after Sarah was helped to go near the vacuum, pull it around the room, turn it on and off, and ride on it. She now felt in control of it. Of course children who are taught how to operate an appliance need to know that it is not a toy and should not be used without supervision.

One other approach is very useful in helping to curtail a child's fear before it becomes strong. This approach is called *bibliotherapy*—or "using books" to help people with their problems. This method involves being watchful of budding or likely fears, selecting appropriate reading material, and discussing it with the child either while reading it to him/her or after the child has read it.[44]

Books can provide explanations which remedy misconceptions or describe the unknown. A child who is afraid that "lions will jump on me and eat me up" will find out that the only lions within thousands of miles are in the zoo and circus, where they are kept in protected areas. Books can help children realize that others have the same feelings. This gives the reader a sense of not being alone and reassures the child that "it's OK to be afraid sometimes." Also, reading nonthreatening stories about the objects or situations that the child ordinarily finds fearful provides a springboard for parent-child sharing of feelings and open communication.

When should you introduce these reading materials? Although books may be used to prevent certain fears from developing if you can anticipate difficulties, many specific fears are not predictable. If you are watchful of the child's wariness and worries, you can present appropriate books as soon as the fear starts.

How do you know what reading materials to select? Suggestions for materials that are useful for specific fears are given in this book, particularly in Chapter 8. If you need additional suggestions, most librarians who staff the children's sections of public libraries will be able to help. You will want materials that relate to the child's fear, but they need not have identical circumstances.

You will also want the books to be ones the child will enjoy. To select enjoyable materials, you should consider the kinds of books and stories the child generally likes. Reading preferences tend to change as children grow older. From about age two or three to six or seven, children like to have stories read to them that relate to familiar events, like going shopping, to school, or to the beach. Then until the age of ten or eleven years, children show great interest in fantasy stories. In late childhood and early adolescence, they tend to like stories about adventure, animals, mystery, sports, and the supernatural. In later adolescence, their reading interests move toward stories about teen-age life in general.

Once you have found materials that might be appropriate, read them yourself and examine the illustrations, trying to think about the book as the child will. If you see potential misconceptions or fearful situations for the child, prepare some explanations and dialogue to use with the child. If there are problems in the material that you cannot effectively prepare for, either change the story line or reject the book. Do not use books that you have not looked at carefully; they can aggravate the fear, rather than reduce it.

Here are some further guidelines:

With a child who is unable to read, when you read the story aloud, call attention to important features of the story and illustrations.

For a young child, a reading session should not last longer than about 30 minutes because of the short attention span; older children can enjoy an hour or so.

During a reading session, be watchful of misunderstandings, wariness, and concerns of the child. Maintain open communication.

A child who can read alone may do so, but time should be set aside when you can discuss the reading together, perhaps at dinner. Try not to be judgmental or preachy about what the child thinks or feels. Instead, help to guide the child's ideas.

Books may be reread many times, especially with a young child, so that the story will be absorbed and understood.

To summarize the methods described in this section, fears can be nipped in the bud using any or all of these methods: teaching relevant skills; maintaining open communication by sharing your own experiences, listening to and understanding what the child says, answering "What if. . . ?" questions, and discussing dreams; giving explanations of things the child misunderstands; helping the child feel in control of the feared object; and using books to help the child cope.

Children who are helped early in dealing with the fears they begin to experience will learn appropriate and effective ways to master fears on their own. As they grow older, they become confident that "I can handle it" when they encounter new challenges.

Identifying the Object of Fear

Anita's parents took her to see *Raiders of the Lost Ark*, the popular movie that contained lengthy and terrifying scenes in a snake pit. She began to cry, as several other young children did, when close-up shots showed the snakes hissing and bearing their fangs. Even adults in the audience made exclamations that reflected fear and revulsion, and the all-powerful stars of the movie were frightened. Her parents thought nothing more than "Oh, poor baby" of her distress.

Later that afternoon Anita was playing in the garage when, without noticing, she brushed against a garden hose hanging on the wall, and the free end of the hose bobbed up and down. When she glimpsed it out of the corner of her eye, she shrieked and ran to her mother. She was so terrified that she couldn't even tell her mother what she was thinking: "There's a snake in the garage, and it tried to get me." By the time she calmed down, her mother had stopped asking "What's wrong" and thought "Well, it's past now."

Sometimes children can't tell you what's wrong. In Anita's case, she was too upset to answer her mother's question. Her mother would have handled this problem better if she had soothed Anita, waited until she had calmed down to ask what was wrong, and gone with the child to see what frightened her—this last step should be done calmly and at the child's own pace. You need to identify what actually happened if you are to show her convincingly that it was not a snake, but a hose.

One problem with trying to identify the object of young children's fears is that they may lack the verbal ability to articulate exactly what is frightening. This can be very frustrating to both the child and the parent. Obviously, to identify the object of fear in this event, you must be flexible, inventive, and patient. If possible, see if the child can *show* you what it is, or use *whatever words* or *pantomime* he or she can. Another approach is to watch for when and where the child appears fearful, and then try to figure out what the object is.

In some cases the child may not be aware of exactly what the feared object is. The source of fear is simply not available to the child's conscious mind. With respect to our interest in identifying the object, it probably doesn't matter whether the memory was purged by way of repression or whether it was "just forgotten." If the parent-child relationship is characterized by open communication and the child still can't specify what the trouble is, your best approach would be to treat the situation as though the child simply lacked the verbal ability to articulate the problem. Try to identify the object of fear from your observations of when and where the child shows fear.

Keeping a log of where and when fear is aroused is very helpful because you can make comparisons and see if there is a pattern or a common thread that ties several fearful situations together. Remember the case in Chapter 2 of an infant named Tony who became distressed whenever he saw a red door. His mother was very puzzled by his reaction, but she eventually put the pieces together when the red doors in the different fearful situations flashed into her mind. Her identification of the object of fear—the red door, stemming from the door at the pediatrician's office—would have been easier if she had kept a record of these events.

For children who can determine the object of their fear and have the verbal skills to describe it, their willingness and opportunity to express it provide the key. One approach that can give children (and even adults) the opportunity and encouragement to identify their fears is a complete-the-sentence activity.[45]

Sit down with the child occasionally in a nondistracting and comfortable place, and explain that you will play a "game" in which you will say part of a sentence, and then each of you will finish the sentence in your own way.

Examples of unfinished sentences are:

1. The people I like best are . . .
2. I wish . . .
3. The thing that scares me a lot is . . .
4. I get angry when . . .
5. I worry when . . .
6. One thing that makes me very happy is . . .

Let the child answer each question first, and then you give yours. Then talk about the reasons for the answers given. Be patient, accepting, and understanding of whatever the child says so that you can maintain open communication.

Try to focus on the child's feelings about the answers he or she gives, and how serious the fears are. If the fears are relatively mild and new, you can probably nip them in the bud using the methods described in the previous section. If the fears are moderately strong and entrenched, you will want also to consider the methods in the next chapter. In either case, use your judgment and creativity to tailor the methods you feel will work to meet the child's needs.

7

Reducing a Child's Fears

"Fighting fire with fire" can apply to the reduction of fears. As we saw in Chapter 3, many fears develop out of the experiences that children have; they *learn* most of their fears. Since this is so, why shouldn't they be able to "unlearn" fear?

METHODS THAT WORK

You can arrange new experiences that allow the child to learn *not* to be afraid in the situations that arouse fear, using the learning and thinking processes that we saw in Chapters 3 and 4: *classical conditioning, imagination, observational learning,* and *reward*.

Conditioning

Remember the infant boy named Little Albert who was conditioned to fear a gentle white rat? A few years later a boy named Peter, who was almost three years old, underwent a psychological evaluation while he was at an institution for the temporary care of children.[46] This evaluation showed that Peter had acquired in his everyday life a fear very much like Albert's—Peter was extremely afraid of furry objects.

> MARCH 10, 10:15 A.M. Peter in high chair, eating candy. Experimenter entered room with a rabbit in an open-meshed wire cage. The rabbit was placed on the table four feet from Peter who immediately began to cry, insisting that the rabbit be taken away. Continued crying until the rabbit was put down 20 feet away. He then started again on the candy, but continued to fuss, "I want you to put Bunny outside." After three minutes he once more burst into tears; the rabbit was removed.

After the next several weeks in which Peter received therapy once or twice daily, his fear diminished.

> APRIL 29, 9:55 A.M. Peter standing in high chair, looking out of the window. He inquired, "Where is the rabbit?" The rabbit was put down on the chair at Peter's feet. Peter patted him, tried to pick him up, but finding the rabbit too heavy asked the experimenter to help in lifting him to the window sill, where he played with him for several minutes.

A remarkable change—how was the fear "unlearned?" One of the critical aspects of Peter's therapy was that the rabbit was *gradually* brought closer and closer without anything unpleasant happening. Research in the many years since this study was done has produced a general rule for using conditioning to help reduce fears: *Arrange for the child to confront the source of fear in gradual steps accompanied by pleasant events* (or, at least, *not un*pleasant events). Because this approach *reverses* the previous learning of a fear reaction, it is called *counterconditioning*.

There are two parts to the method of counterconditioning that you must arrange: (1) the gradual steps and (2) the pleasant events. Let's start with the *pleasant events*. During the sessions for counterconditioning or unlearning a fear, the child should feel calm, relaxed, comfortable, and happy. Make use of anything you think will produce these feelings in the child you are trying to help. Here are some suggestions:

Try to make the "session" seem like a game. Although you will have an underlying structure for it, each session can be introduced and run in a casual and free-flowing way. The more formal a session seems, the less relaxed the child will be.

Have at least one person present with whom the child feels safe and comfortable. The parents are usually good choices.

If possible, use familiar surroundings for the sessions, particularly with infants and preschoolers.

If the child has a "security blanket" or other such items, have them available.

Often you can conduct counterconditioning while the child is engaged in other activities, such as watching a favorite TV show, listening to enjoyable music, playing with toys, or eating delicious foods. For instance, for Peter's fear the rabbit was moved closer and closer while he sat in a high chair eating candy.

Children who have trouble getting comfortable and calm for a session can be *trained to relax* by doing some muscle exercises. These relaxation exercises are easy and fun to do, and simply involve alternating the tensing and releasing of specific muscle groups. You can call these exercises the "Floppy Game," showing the child that the arms and legs flop down when the muscles are relaxed. A rag doll, such as Raggedy Ann or Andy, is great for showing "how floppy you can be when you relax your muscles."

When you play the Floppy Game, pick a quiet and non-distracting place where you can sit in comfortable chairs or lie down on the floor together. Do the exercises with the child. (You can probably use the relaxation too!) For some children, getting them to relax with the Floppy Game will be relatively easy—all you'll have to do is "talk" them into relaxing. Using a slow and soothing voice, you can repeat several times, "Your whole body is loose and free, and you feel calm and quiet. Your arms and legs are just lying there all floppy, just like the rag doll I showed you before. Your face, and neck, and even your tummy are all floppy too. You feel good."

Other children will not relax very easily just with this introduction. Their bodies will still be stiff, and they will need to do the tensing and releasing exercises. The following commands describe a series of these exercises, each of which may be repeated two or three times in a relaxation session.

1. "OK. Let's raise our arms and put them out in front. Now make a fist with both your hands, really hard. Hold the fist tight and you will see how your muscles in your hands and arms feel when they are tight." (hold for 7–10 seconds)

    "That's very good. Now, when I say relax, I want the muscles in your hands and arms to become floppy, like the rag doll, and your arms will drop to your sides. OK, relax." (about 15 seconds)

2. "Let's raise our legs out in front of us. Now tighten the muscles in your feet and legs, really hard. Make the muscles really tight, and hold it." (7–10 seconds)

    "Very good. Now relax the muscles in your feet and legs, and let them flop to the floor. They feel so good. So calm and relaxed." (15 seconds)

3. "Now let's do our tummy muscles. Tighten your tummy, really hard—and hold it." (7–10 seconds)

"OK. Relax your tummy, and feel how good it feels. So comfortable." (15 seconds)

4. "Leave your arms at your side, but tighten the muscles in your shoulders and neck. You can do this by moving your shoulders up toward your head. Hold the muscles very tightly in your shoulders and neck." (7–10 seconds)

"Now relax those muscles so they are floppy, and see how good that feels." (15 seconds)

5. "Let's tighten the muscles in our faces. Scrunch up your whole face so that all of the muscles are tight—the muscles in your cheeks, and your mouth, and your nose, and your forehead. Really scrunch up your face, and hold it." (7–10 seconds)

"Now relax all the muscles in your face—your cheeks, mouth, nose, and forehead. Feel how nice that is." (15 seconds)

6. "Now I want us to take a very, very deep breath—so deep that there's no more room inside for more air. Hold the air in." (use a shorter time: 6–8 seconds)

"That's good. Now slowly let the air out. Very slowly, until it's all out." (hold *only a couple of seconds* because it may become uncomfortable) "And now breathe as you usually do." (15 seconds)

Some children don't really relax their muscles when you first tell them to. Instead of letting the arms or legs *fall* down, they *move* them down. If this happens, show the child how to make them floppy. Another thing that some children do that should be corrected is to tense more muscles than they are asked to. For example, when asked to make a fist they may tighten some facial muscles. So, the first time you do these exercises, make sure the child is tensing only the muscles named.

After a few practice sessions, these exercises become increasingly effective in relaxing children. The child can then be instructed to do the exercises at least once or twice a day, such as before going to sleep at night. Eventually the child will be able to do one or two of the exercises almost anywhere—in any position—anytime there is a tense situation. Relaxation can become almost second nature, and it will help to reduce tension in fearful encounters.

Now that you have several ways to make the counter-conditioning session reasonably pleasant and comfortable, we need to see how to arrange the *gradual steps* that will help the child contact the source of a fear. Suppose you wanted to help a ten-year-old girl named Sue overcome a phobia of fire (pyrophobia) she developed after she witnessed a fire in which two children were burned to death. At first she seemed unaffected by this experience, but a few days later she began to avoid such things as matches, candles, and stoves even when turned off.

By talking with Sue, observing when she shows fear, and using common sense, you could devise a series of 10 to 15 gradual steps that are rank-ordered from least to most fearful for *her*. These steps would consist of fire-related situations, that might start with a matchbook placed on a table and end with Sue tending a fire. For example:

1. Matchbook on a table, 10 feet away from Sue (no fire).
2. Kitchen stove off, 2 feet away.
3. Matchbook on a table, 3 feet away (no fire).
4. Visible candle burning in the next room.
5. Burning candle in the same room she is in, 10 feet away.
6. Oven of stove is on, 3 feet away, but she can't see the flame.
7. Burning candle, 4 feet away.
8. Kitchen stove burner-flame on (moderate setting), 10 feet away.
9. Stove burner-flame on (high setting), 3 feet away.
10. Small fire in the fireplace, 10 feet away.
11. Sue turns stove burner on and off.

12. While stove is on, Sue tends a pot and moves it to another burner.
13. Large fire in the fireplace, 8 feet away.
14. Large fire in the fireplace, 3 feet away.
15. Sue pokes burning logs with fireplace tools.

To construct a series of gradual steps like this one, *start with more than you'll need*—perhaps 18 or 20. Then, continuing to use your common sense and your observations of and talks with the child, pare the steps down to 10 or 15.

Start paring by setting up "anchor points"—the least fearful step and the most fearful step of the original set. Make sure that the most fearful step is a reasonable goal to achieve; it should be an activity that (1) people ordinarily do, (2) the child has the skills and physical ability to do, and (3) is not very dangerous. Rank order the remaining original steps—the ones in between the anchor points—and cull out about 5, using these same three criteria and one more: try to equalize the "size" of the steps as much as possible.

What does it mean to "equalize the size of the steps?" When you rank the steps on the basis of fearfulness, each succeeding step will be more fear-arousing than the preceding one. To make the series of steps *gradual*, the "distance" between steps should be fairly consistent through the entire series. At least, there should be no extremely large gaps for the child to bridge.

For instance, in the steps for the fire phobia a large gap would have occurred if the first 5 or 6 steps involved no fire (matchbooks in various locations) and step 7 had Sue facing a raging fire, 3 feet away. A gap this large is likely to be extremely difficult for the child, and she might even refuse to participate in this or any other activities you suggest to reduce her fear.

Once you have constructed the gradual steps, the procedure for doing the counterconditioning is fairly straightforward. Make sure the child is calm, relaxed, comfortable, and happy, using the suggestions we saw a little earlier. Then *begin with the least fearful of the gradual steps*. If you were trying to help Sue with her fire phobia, you would go to a table, 10 feet away from her, produce a matchbook, and have her watch you place it on the table.

Then you would sit near Sue and carefully watch her reaction to this situation. Her initial reaction might be one of wariness, looking over at the matchbook occasionally as if she expected it might do something spontaneously. Eventually, however, this wariness will begin to decline. The "pleasant events," such as her parents, toys, and favorite music being there, and your soothing voice encouraging her to relax, should help overcome the initial wariness.

After she has shown no sign of fear for a few minutes and agrees that "It doesn't bother me anymore," the counterconditioning can move to the next step in the series. Note: *do not use a new step if she was still afraid at the previous one, or if the new step arouses a strong fear response*. This judgment should always be based on the child's reaction. If the new step is too frightening, the gap is probably too large. You will need to revise the set of gradual steps by finding and using an additional step that allows a smaller gap. Don't force the child to any step.

In addition to these procedures for counterconditioning, the following guidelines are important:

Reducing a moderately strong fear is likely to take several sessions, each being 15–30 minutes long.

Don't rush the child—let the sessions progress at *her* pace.

Try to have each session end on a positive note: successfully overcoming a step in the series. If you think the next step is not likely to be completed successfully before the session is over, reserve it for next time.

The first step you use in each session should be one that the child has already overcome. Typically, this step will be the last one completed in the previous session. Go through this step as though you had not done it before, until the child shows no fear and agrees to move on.

Always be flexible and be willing to revise the procedure to meet the child's needs. Your plan may have a flaw, or circumstances between sessions may change the child's fear. For example, Sue might see a "fire-eater" on TV and decide that "Fires aren't always dangerous," or she may hear about another fire-related disaster that could "rekindle" her fear.

Write down the steps you are planning to use on individual slips of paper or cards so that you can rearrange them and cull out some. Keep a log of what occurred during each session, especially if there will be a long period of time between sessions. Use this to make a chart showing her progress.

The gradual steps we have seen so far involve *real-life* contacts, of varying degrees, with objects or situations that relate to the fear. Generally speaking, real-life contacts are an important and effective ingredient in the counterconditioning process.

One circumstance that rules out real-life contacts is when the object of fear doesn't exist, as with the fear of ghosts or witches. Another circumstance is when the fear is so strong that *any* degree of real-life contact is very frightening. As a result, you will not have a beginning step in the series that the child can tolerate. In such circumstances, at least part of the series of gradual steps should involve "non-real-life" situations.[47]

How do you incorporate non-real-life situations in the series of gradual steps? There are two ways: (1) You can use one or more steps that involve *symbolic* situations by showing pictures, films, or models of the fear-related object. For example, with a boy who is extremely afraid of cats, the first few steps in the series might have him look at picture books or cartoons with cats, and a toy cat. (2)

You can also use steps that involve *imagined* situations, by having the child imagine a scene that has a cat, and perhaps himself and/or other characters coming into pleasant and successful contact with the cat.

Alison, the daughter of a friend and colleague of mine, was somewhat anxious at nursery school and developed a problem: she wouldn't eat or drink any food whatsoever unless her mother was present. To help Alison overcome this problem, my friend used a counterconditioning plan that began with imagined situations. For instance, Alison was asked to "think about taking a fast lick of an ice cream cone at school." Later, she was able to handle real-life gradual steps, such as opening her lunch box. The plan worked beautifully.

The conditioning procedures we have seen in this section are highly effective, and have been used successfully with a wide variety of children's fears, such as of the dark, insects, high places, and water.[48] The other methods for unlearning fear that I am about to describe are also effective, and they can be used in combination with conditioning procedures. Once again, you may pick from all of these methods to tailor a plan that you think will work best for a particular child's problem.

Imagination

The child's imagination can be used to help overcome fears through fantasies, storytelling, and "Let's Pretend" games. One example is the case of an eight-year-old boy who was afraid of the dentist.[49] Using Batman and Robin as heroes, the boy was asked to imagine his heroes visiting the dentist while he watched them receive dental treatment, and then to imagine himself in the dentist's chair while Batman and Robin stood by. After practicing this fantasy several times a day for a week, the boy was able to go to the dentist and sit through four fillings without flinching.

Observational Learning

Children learn many of their fears by observing what other people do, but they can also learn *not* to be afraid in the same way.

Very often childhood fears that become "outgrown" do so in two ways: (1) the child encounters the feared object, such as a dog, and nothing bad happens and (2) the child *observes* other people, especially playmates, in the feared situation, and they are calm and able to deal with it. The first way is essentially an everyday counterconditioning process; and the second way is an everyday observational learning process. The risk you take in letting these processes "happen" on their own was described in the Chapter 5 section called "What if You Do Nothing?" What I advocate, of course, is that you guide the processes so they will happen in a careful and effective way. Doing nothing may allow backfiring that aggravates the fear.

By observing a fearless individual in a problem situation, children can learn the relevant skills they need, for example, to handle animals, to swim, or to interact with their age-mates. At the same time, a fearless individual can show that the situation is not as dangerous as they thought.

One way that observational learning can be used is *symbolically,* through films, picture books, and the like. Picture books are easy to get, and your local librarian may be able to suggest appropriate ones. Films are more difficult to come by, and you need equipment to show them. Therapists have used films of fearless children successfully to reduce a variety of childhood fears, such as of dentists, doctors, snakes, and social interaction.[50] Observational learning by way of a symbolic approach can be effective for many children, but "there's nothing like the real thing." If the fear is fairly strong, a symbolic approach may be most useful as a starting point or launching pad for getting the child to observe a real-life situation.

Observational learning, using *real-life* feared objects, is a very effective process for reducing fear, especially when it encourages the child to *join in* and *gradually contact* the feared object. This approach was the primary one used by the parents of six-year-old Brian who was quite fearful of snakes. Let's see what they did.

Fortunately Brian's parents were not afraid of nonpoisonous snakes—they weren't "fond" of snakes, but they could touch them calmly, straightforwardly, and without appearing repelled. They bought a small nonpoisonous snake and a cage which they kept outside the house. They took some Polaroid pictures of the snake: one with objects nearby that Brian was familiar with so that he could see in the picture how big it was; another with his mother sitting next to the cage, smiling while looking at the snake; another with her touching the snake. They also bought a toy snake. Brian's parents began the observational learning process with a symbolic approach because he was too frightened of snakes to watch a real one, even from a distance.

Now they were ready to help reduce Brian's fear. They started with the toy snake. They sat down with him in the house and told him they had a *toy* snake in a box on the other side of the room. His father said, "Now I want you to watch me," as he walked to the toy snake, opened the box, and picked it up. His mother sat next to him, and as Father shook the toy, tossed it into the air, and caught it, Mother said, "See it's just a little toy. It's not a real one and it can't move or do anything by itself." Father then put the toy on the floor several feet from Brian, and both parents petted it while the boy watched. Next, his parents encouraged him to come closer and closer, a little at a time. In a short while, he was able to pet it, and then he was able to imitate his parents' actions—picking up the toy snake, jiggling it, and tossing and catching it.

The next day Brian's parents used the toy snake again, and he was able to play with it almost immediately. When he seemed comfortable with it, his parents got him to help name it, which he did: "Snoopy Snake." And his mother responded, "Snoopy Snake. That's a wonderful name for a snake. In fact I know a real snake named Snoopy." While Father went outside to set up the cage in the back yard, Mother talked to Brian about the real Snoopy Snake and how he eats insects and worms—and she showed him the Polaroid photos of the snake. She had also learned enough about snakes to talk about poisonous and nonpoisonous ones and answer his questions, like "Where do they live?"

Then she walked over to a window from which the cage could be seen, called Brian to her, held him on her lap, pointed and said: "Why, there's the real Snoopy Snake now. He's inside the cage all locked up and can't get out unless we want him to. He's a nice snake, the kind that can't hurt people. Daddy knows Snoopy Snake too, and likes him.

"Oh," she continued, "I think Daddy asked Snoopy Snake if he'd like to come out and play for a little while." They sat and watched as Father carefully opened the lock on the cage, reached in, and picked up the snake. He held it for a while, let it crawl around his hands for a few minutes, put it back in the cage, and made sure Brian could see that it was now locked. Mother noted: "See. Snoopy Snake is locked up in the cage again, and he can't get out unless we want him to. Why don't we go outside so we can see Snoopy Snake better?"

Brian didn't like that idea. His mother said "OK. Maybe you'll want to try it later. Then, if you want to, I'll go with you and we can sit anywhere you want."

Later on Mother asked, "Have you thought about where you would sit if you went outside?" Brian answered, "Yes, way over there by the fence." Mother replied, "I'd like to do that too. Come on—I'll take you out there and you can sit on my lap."

From that location they watched as Father played with it

again and put it back in the cage. The parents now switched roles—Father sat with Brian while Mother played with the snake. The parents praised Brian's progress, saying "I'm glad to see that you could sit outside today and watch us play with Snoopy Snake."

The next morning, Brian was willing to go outside and watch his father play with the snake again, and he was even willing to sit a little closer. Whenever he was ready, Mother moved him closer. In about 30 minutes, when he was only three feet from the snake, his parents decided to have an intermission for an hour or so. They praised him again for his progress.

When they resumed the process, Brian was still willing to sit close to the snake. The next goal was to get him to touch it, and they did this in three steps. First they had him hold Mother's left hand while she petted the snake with her other hand. Then they got him to imitate touching it while wearing a glove. Finally he could touch it with his bare hand.

As you can see, real-life observational learning with gradual contact with the feared object is similar to the gradual steps used in counterconditioning. The most important difference between these methods is that another person is observed fearlessly dealing with the problem situation.

When you design an observational learning plan to reduce a child's fear, keep in mind the material on counterconditioning and the following suggestions:

Carefully *select the person* whom the child will observe. It should be someone who is *reasonably fearless and competent* in the fearful situation, and whom the child will be inclined to imitate—prime candidates are the *parents* or other children about the same age as the fearful child.

Be certain that *nothing negative* is likely to happen to the person the child watches. As an obvious example, if you were showing a child who is afraid of heights how safe it is to climb a ladder, make sure the ladder is sturdy and securely positioned. If you were careless about these things, you would be setting a poor example for safe ladder use—and if you fall. . . .

Although the person the child watches should be *reasonably* competent and fearless, it is usually not harmful for the model to show some caution or apprehension while coping with the situation. Fearful children often will not look at someone who takes bold action, and are likely to think "She can do that without fear because she's so good at it. I'm not!"

Have the child observe *two or more persons*, individually, coping with the feared situation. If only one person is watched, the child might assume that the model has special talents that rule out fear. The child is more likely to conclude "Maybe I can do that too" if several models are observed.

Try to use a variety of related feared-objects, such as snakes of different color and size.

Praise the child for progress made.

Help the child to keep written records of progress. You can jointly make a chart; for instance, using gold stars to show how close Brian got to Snoopy Snake. This shows him that progress is being made toward ridding him of the fear, and it encourages him to keep on trying.

Reward

Are rewards useful in reducing children's fears? To some extent, yes. For one thing, children are usually eager to shed their fears. Successfully doing so is rewarding, especially if children see their progress in black and white on a chart. Also, successfully overcoming fear takes effort, and children—like adults—want praise and recognition for their accomplishments.

Promising children rewards, such as money, candy, or watching extra TV, for their efforts and successes in reducing fear seems to have limited or mixed value. Sometimes it can help, but there are three difficulties:

1. You must select a reward the *child really wants*.
2. You must *not require too much improvement* all at once. For instance, promising a reward to a boy who is afraid of the dark "if you go to bed and don't make a peep all night" is requiring far too much. A more effective approach would be to reward him for increased lengths of time in the dark, beginning with a very short time.
3. Rewards should be given to the child *for reducing his fear, not just for failing to express it*. Failing to express it might simply reflect a covering-up process, rather than an unlearning process. It is especially difficult to tell whether his improvement is a cover-up if you cannot detect subtle signs of distress, for instance, in the dark.

A FEW NOTES ABOUT REDUCING FEARS

"What does it *mean* if you're afraid of snakes?" a woman asked me a couple of years ago. There was a time when many psychologists thought that a fear of snakes almost always meant something about the person's sexual and personality adjustment, because of the phallic symbolism. This woman's question reflects the popular notion that there is a universal underlying psychological meaning to all personality and adjustment problems.

Although this kind of underlying meaning may apply in

some individual cases, for most people who are afraid of snakes their fear simply means that they learned that snakes can bite you and poison you with their fangs and that snakes are slimy and disgusting.

Sometimes the object of a fear is, in fact, symbolic of or related to the original source of the fear, but the person has repressed the source because of feelings of guilt and shame. George began to masturbate when he was nine years old, but he had been told not to "play with yourself." Later he learned the name for this act, and that "it is vile and evil, and will make you sterile." He was also told that "people will be able to tell that you do it" from certain telltale signs, such as hair growing on your palms. He worried a lot about this.

In adolescence, George developed an aversion to young women, became asexual—he no longer had any interest in sex or sexual matters—and he had a mysterious fear of boats. Why boats? Because when he was nine and first started to masturbate, his parents kept a cabin cruiser docked near their home, and that's where he went to "do it."

Although identifying the source of George's problem is useful in preventing his fears from becoming more numerous and intense, understanding where the problem began is usually not enough to overcome the fears it already spawned. Many people can describe the circumstances and relationships behind their fears, and yet continue to be anxious and afraid. The methods we have described in this chapter will still be needed to help George overcome his fear of women and boats.

One very important and encouraging *dividend* of reducing a child's fear is that he or she will tend to become better able to cope with other fears that you have not worked on yet. This results partly from an increased sense of self-confidence and belief that "I can handle things that frighten me." An adult client put this into words neatly: "The biggest benefit to me of the . . . treatment was the feeling that if I could lick snakes, I could lick anything. It gave me the confidence to tackle, also successfully, some personal stuff.''[51]

Helping a child overcome fears is a good investment. The earlier you start, the easier it will be—and the dividends will be greater.

SEEKING PROFESSIONAL HELP

Only a small percentage of children enter professional therapy to help them overcome severely disabling fears.[52] Although we don't know how many children suffer disabling fears without receiving the help they need, their ranks are probably large. They go without treatment for many reasons: insufficient services in their locale, their parents can't afford the costs, all the relatives say ''It's just a phase—he'll grow out of it,'' and so on.

If you use the methods described in this book to prevent fears, and reduce those that become strong, it is highly unlikely that your child will need therapy. But if the child does, how will you tell that professional therapy is needed and how do you find a good therapist?

When Do Fears Need Therapy?

As you undoubtedly expect, answering this question is not as straightforward as a medical diagnosis can be. Psychologists do not have tests to reach a measurable conclusion that ''His fear count has reached a dangerous level and is endangering his well-being.'' In a small number of extreme cases the need for therapy is obvious, but what about all the others?

Probably the best way for you to reach a tentative conclusion is to do what Alice's parents did—they examined her problem applying the following questions:

Does Alice have many fears and seem almost to be "afraid of everything?"

Does she have only one or two very strong fears, but they are serious enough to interfere with the entire family's activities? An example would be if her fear of animals made it impossible for anyone to go to the zoo.

Do her fears seem to be interfering with her social relationships and schoolwork?

Does she seem to be a generally unhappy child?

Are her fears "driving everyone else crazy?" An example would be if, every half hour, she washes her hands because of her phobia of germs or she checks that the windows and doors are locked because she is afraid something will enter the house.

Is she often anxious or fearful, but unable or unwilling to describe what's bothering her?

Does she suffer from a physical condition, such as heart trouble, asthma, headaches, ulcers, or colitis, that is aggravated by emotional stress?

Have some of her fears persisted or gotten worse for a long time, perhaps more than a year?

Have you tried to use the methods I describe in this book, and not had success?

Are there persistent family difficulties, such as marital instability (frequent arguments, separation, or divorce), parental drug or alcohol abuse, or child abuse?

If the answer to at least one of these ten questions is an emphatic *yes* or if the answer to *several questions is at least a* qualified *yes,* you should consider professional therapy.

Pursuing the Issue of Therapy

If you decide to consider therapy for the child, you will want to get professional advice. Does the child really need therapy? Where should you look? How do you find a therapist who can help your child?

You can get advice and helpful information from several sources:

1. Your pediatrician or family physician is a good place to start. If the problem seems serious to the physician, he or she may want to give the child a medical checkup before advising you or making a referral. Many symptoms of fear and anxiety can result from physical disorders.
2. Your child's school probably has a psychologist or counselor who may be able to advise you and suggest appropriate therapists.
3. Members of the clergy often have information about therapists.
4. Community or county mental health centers generally have listings of qualified therapists. You will find these centers listed in the phone book, usually under the name of the community, or under "Mental Health . . .", or in the classified directory under "Guide to Human Services."

After you have consulted these sources, you will probably know with reasonable certainty whether the child needs therapy. If you decide that he or she does, and you have gathered some names of therapists, you should make a selection on the basis of several factors:

1. Try to find a therapist who specializes, or has considerable experience, in *childhood* problems.

2. You may need to choose between a psychologist or a psychiatrist. Clinical psychologists generally have had more extensive training in psychology, but psychiatrists are medical doctors and can prescribe medication. Many psychologists work with physicians so that drugs may be prescribed if needed.

3. Check the therapist's credentials with local branches of the following organizations:

   The National Association of Mental Health
     1800 North Kent Street
     Arlington, Virginia 22209
   The American Psychological Association
     1200 17th Street N.W.
     Washington, D.C. 20036
   The American Psychiatric Association
     1700 18th Street N.W.
     Washington, D.C. 20009

   The requirements to practice psychotherapy differ from state to state. Just because someone has an office and a practice, you shouldn't automatically assume he or she has had appropriate training.

4. Try to determine whether the therapist uses a variety of approaches, especially those described in this book. For the reduction of fear, counterconditioning (sometimes referred to as "desensitization") and observational learning (also called "modeling" or "social learning") methods are extremely effective.

5. Don't be reluctant to shop around a bit, considering the fees and the likelihood that the therapist and the child will "get along."

This chapter was designed to give you the tools to help children with their fears and to give enough information so that you will understand when to do what and why. The general principles were described with specific examples so that you can tailor the methods you use to the needs of the child.

The remainder of this book presents specific applications of these methods to particular cases of common childhood fears.

8

Case Studies

Helping Children Cope with 15 Common Fears

Now that you have read the earlier chapters of this book you are ready to apply your knowledge toward helping children cope. You know what fears are, the ones children tend to have at different ages, and ways to prevent and reduce them.

This chapter examines fifteen of the most common types of fears children have. I have organized them roughly by the age when they tend to become prominent. These fears relate to:

As you use these suggestions, keep in mind that your circumstances will require you to change the methods occasionally. My suggestions are not meant to give you a single "prescription" for all children. Each child is different from the next and will need special changes or adjustments in the methods.

In making such adjustments, use the knowledge you've gained from earlier chapters, your judgment and experience with the particular child, and your own creativity. You can and should design a somewhat unique procedure with mine as a base. Consult Chapters 6 and 7 so you will design and apply your procedure well.

One more thing. Suppose you have just finished helping a child overcome a moderately strong fear. Your job is not really over. Now is the time to look at the section on preventing and "nipping" the fear to see how you can prevent a "relapse." A child who can now cope with a previously feared situation is not necessarily "immune."

FEAR OF STRANGERS

Not long ago people thought that all babies develop a fear of strangers sometime between five and twelve months of age. Some psychologists thought that it was a universal and regular developmental milestone—as inevitable as walking and talking—so they named it the "eight-month anxiety." Today we know that not all babies become fearful of strangers. And there are easy things parents can do to help babies feel more comfortable with new people.

Preventing and Nipping the Fear

Babies aren't the only people who are wary of strangers—you probably are too. Think about how you feel while walking through a "dangerous neighborhood," looking suspiciously at perfectly nice and harmless people. Or how about your feelings at a party where you don't know many people? Remembering this will help you be sensitive to the baby's concerns around unfamiliar people—even Grandma!

Since infants don't show fear reactions to unfamiliar people before the age of five months, there's lots of time to prevent this fear from developing. Mostly what you need to do is give the baby experiences with a variety of people under comfortable, nonthreatening circumstances.

A good time to start is when the infant reaches about three months of age. By that age the vision of infants has sharpened, and they pay a lot more attention to people's faces—especially the eyes and mouth. Also, infants are awake much longer at three months than when they were younger.

The baby is likely to be comfortable at home and in the mother's or father's arms while the parent has a calm and pleasant conversation with a friend, the "stranger." When a friend comes over to the house and the baby's awake, keep the child with you if you can. Explain to the friend that you want to help the baby get used to people gradually.

Seat the "stranger" at a distance initially, perhaps at the far end of the sofa on which you are sitting. Hold the baby so that he or she can look at the stranger and at you. As you chat, check to see how the baby is responding to the stranger's presence. Does the baby look at this person? Is the baby attentive and calm? If so, have the stranger move a little closer. Continue the procedure of assessing the baby's reaction and moving closer until the stranger is at a comfortable distance, perhaps three feet from the baby.

The friend doesn't need to make any special fuss with the baby. Just chatting with you will do fine. The baby simply needs to become accustomed to new people. Variety is important, so follow this procedure with a few friends. As you can see, the technique doesn't need to interfere with everyone having a casual and enjoyable visit.

When you feel the baby is ready, you may gradually extend the procedure to bring friends in social contact with the baby. This can begin with these familiar people just smiling and directing baby talk at the infant. Then they could touch the baby gently, and soon pick up the infant with the parent close by and in full view. It is especially important to use a gradual introduction to strangers if the baby has a "difficult" temperament.[53]

Sometimes parents allow friends or relatives—who are strangers to the baby—to introduce themselves when neither parent is in view. "Ginny's in her crib. Go on in and say hello. I'll be along in a minute," the parent may say. This can be a mistake, unless the child has had a lot of positive experiences with people and you know she'll handle it well.

Other things you can do to help the baby feel comfortable with strangers are:

Take the infant places where there are strangers, such as when you go shopping or on a recreational outing.
Take the baby places where there are other infants or toddlers. If old enough to creep or walk, allow the baby to approach other children with you nearby.
When strangers are around, pick up or stay in view and close to the baby.

Watch for the well meaning, but not sensitive, person who will rush up to the infant to be friendly. If you see this coming, intervene pleasantly by striking up a little conversation and asking the person to make overtures gradually.

Although you may feel a bit embarrassed if the baby begins to react negatively to a relative, your understanding of the baby's point of view should help you intervene in a positive way. Remember, it's not how well *you* know the person that counts to the infant.

Reducing the Fear

At fourteen months of age, Debbie's fear of strangers was getting worse. She was the first child of parents who worked almost 7 days a week. They ran a fledgling mail-order business out of their home. Because one parent could always be home to care for her while the other was out running errands, she didn't get out of the house much and met very few people. Friends and relatives came to visit Debbie's parents occasionally, but usually at night when she was already in bed.

Once Debbie's parents realized she had a problem, they got professional advice and helped her overcome her fear. The procedure they used consisted of counterconditioning and observational learning. For part of the process, they invited her grandparents to come for a week's visit, which the parents had wanted to do soon anyway. The grandparents lived 200 miles away and hadn't seen Debbie in 7 months. When her father invited them, he explained the problem and asked that they refrain from getting near her initially.

The procedure actually started before the grandparents arrived. Debbie's parents got some large photographs of the grandparents and spent time teaching her to name them.

She could say "Nana" for her grandmother's picture and something like "Bamba" for her grandfather's. After their arrival the following gradual steps were used. Debbie:

1. watched her father and grandparents chat while across the room in her mother's arms playing peekaboo.
2. watched as in #1, but at a distance of only 10 feet.
3. watched as in #1, but at 8 feet.
4. watched as in #3, but the parents switched positions and she now saw her mother chat with the grandparents.
5. continued as in #4, and named the grandparents' photographs.
6. continued as in #5, but when she named a grandparent's picture, that person would smile at her and say, "Hi, Debbie."
7. watched as in #1, but at 5 feet.
8. watched as in #7, and her mother pointed at and named her father, grandmother, and grandfather.
9. continued as in #8, but at 4 feet and her mother got her to imitate the three names. When Debbie said a name, that person smiled and said, "That's right, Debbie. I'm _____."
10. played "Give and Take" with her mother and father while in her mother's arms and the grandparents were 4 feet away. (To play this game, the parent hands a toy to the child, then puts out a hand as if to receive it back, says "Thank you" when the baby gives the toy back, and then offers the toy to the baby again.)
11. continued as in #10, but a grandparent sat closer and joined in the game, receiving the toy from the father and then offering it to Debbie. Sometimes when Debbie wouldn't accept it from the grandparent, the mother did and passed it to her.
12. played other games in the group, and occasionally a grandparent would touch her gently and smile.

Each of the steps took between 5 and 15 minutes, and they were spaced over 2 days. On the third day the grandparents were thrilled to hold Debbie in their arms—with Mother near and in view—for the first time since their arrival.

Later in the week, Debbie saw other relatives in her home, mostly from a distance. And she seemed much more comfortable in their presence than she used to be. In the following weeks, her parents introduced her to other people gradually. The parents made sure to help her feel comfortable by using the kinds of ideas I described in the preceding section.

FEAR OF SEPARATION

The loving bond that babies develop for their parents, particularly the mother, is so important and central to children's functioning that the possible loss of this relationship is very frightening to them. This fear begins to show up late in the first year, when most infants get distressed if separated for just a few minutes from the mother. It seems to occur in almost all infants by fifteen months of age, and then diminishes as children get older. For many children the fear of separation or abandonment remains a focal concern at six years of age and beyond.

The increasing ability of children, as they get older, to cope with temporary separations from their parents probably relates to their improved thinking abilities. Older children can better understand the circumstances of the separation, such as why the mother left, where she has gone, and when she'll return. But infants and toddlers don't understand these things and tend to feel abandoned, especially if they are left in an unfamiliar environment with unfamiliar people. No wonder many two-year-olds hold on to their mothers for dear life when they go shopping.

Fear of separation from the parents is such a central issue for infants and young children that it underlies many of their worries and problems. This fear probably contributes to the distress shown in each of the following cases with two- to five-year-old children:

Annie will not leave her own yard by herself because she's afraid she will get lost and not find her way back.

Joey resists going to bed alone, and sobs for his mother.

Bonnie begins to have trouble sleeping after being told that they will be moving to a new house.

Alice became so distressed on her first night at a 2-week summer camp that she was returned home the next day.

Neil cries and clings to his mother while on her lap after being told that he has to go to the hospital for a few days.

Jimmy and his sister Lynn cry themselves to sleep whenever either of their parents must be away on professional trips.

Kathy has a nightmare after hearing her parents quarreling loudly and her father threatening to leave home.

Preventing and Nipping the Fear

How can you help young children cope effectively with their fear of separation? There are many things you can do, beginning in the first year. One of the most important things is to help infants gain a sense of *trust* in others and in themselves.

Babies are dependent on their parents to satisfy their needs—for food and shelter and for love, social contact, and security. If these needs are met with responsive and loving care, children are in a good position to trust their worlds and the relationship they have with their parents. On the other hand, babies whose needs are not met promptly, regularly, and sensitively tend to have trouble trusting their parents and their worlds. These children are apt to feel insecure and fearful of the people and events they encounter.

Infants strive to develop trust in themselves, too—a sense of *competence*. Those who gain a strong feeling of competence are better able to function independently of their parents. As a result, they are less fearful in situations when their parents are not around. Infants and toddlers develop feelings of competence gradually through their experiences. The best experiences are those that encourage children to explore freely and learn independently when they want to, yet have available the security and guidance of their parents when needed. Parents can promote a sense of competence in their children by providing access to toys and people. Try to minimize restrictions by gates and playpens as the child becomes able to locomote.

When the infant reaches six months of age, a good game to play is peekaboo. It helps the baby learn to cope with separation by taking the parent out of view for brief periods, which can be lengthened gradually. The covering of the infant's eyes, or the parent's hiding out of view, is brief enough for babies to experience without fear. Infants usually have a wonderful time with this game. As the baby gets older, you can begin to lengthen the separation period, and even begin to change the game to hide-and-seek.

Another good thing to do periodically is leave the baby alone in a room at home with lots of toys after the child begins to play. You could go into the next room and do some chores, read a book, or watch TV, listening for whether the child really needs you. Gradually you can extend the amount of time the child is alone from several minutes to an hour or more. One way to make being alone easier for the child is to let him or her hear your voice or to pop back into view every now and then. When you do, try to say something that rewards or encourages playing independently.

It's also a good idea to begin leaving the infant at home

with a babysitter fairly early. The first time, don't go out at all. Have the sitter come over for a few hours and help around the house, play with the baby, and so on. (Check the section of this chapter on fear of strangers.) Initially, stay in the same room with them, but try moving away from the baby or going briefly into other rooms. Watch how the child reacts. The second time, have the sitter come over an hour or so before you want to leave to do a few brief errands. Have the sitter stay an extra half-hour after you return. As long as the child shows no serious problem with the separation, keep reducing the amount of time both you and the sitter are there together.

Infant and toddler separation fears that have not become very strong can be nipped in the bud by using some of the following methods.

• Take the child places where there are age-mates to play with. During the second and third years, children playing together engage in more sharing of play materials and more conversation. Encourage the child to socialize and spend less time near you.

• Take the child on overnight visits away from home. At first the child may need to sleep near you, but you can increase the distance and use separate rooms eventually. Take a night light, just in case, even if the child never needed one at home.

• Children can benefit in many ways from high-quality day care on a part-time basis after the first year. If you decide to enroll the child, be sure to make the separation transition gradual.

• Sometimes when parents must go away for a while, the children feel that they are being punished for some wrong. If you suspect this is the case, explain the actual circumstances of the trip.

• Children who fear that their parents may divorce, need to discuss their worries with both parents. Often this is not workable or too difficult for the parents, and a trained counselor may be needed. One of the problems these children often have is a feeling of guilt and responsibility for the marital discord. This is likely if the parents have quarreled about the children and their care.

• Use appropriate children's books for bibliotherapy. Because of the association of separation fear with other problems, I will recommend books for children who fear divorce, going to camp, and becoming lost. *Divorce:* For children in the four to eight age-range, *Daddy* by J. Caines (Harper, 1977) is recommended. It's about a girl's visit with her father after the divorce, and deals with her experiences and feelings. For six- to eight-year-olds, *I Have Two Families* by D. Helmering (Abingdon, 1981). This narrative and picture book describes a girl's feelings and experiences at the mother's and the father's houses. For eight- to twelve-year-olds, *It's Not the End of the World* by J. Blume (Bradbury; Bantam, 1972). Divorce is seen through the eyes of the two children, Karen and Jeff, in a sensibly written and credible story.

Camp: For four- to eight-year-olds, *Katie Goes to Camp* by E. Schick (Macmillan, 1968). Katie's first time at camp is marked by uneasiness, but also fun. For eight- to twelve-year-olds, *The Cool Kids' Guide to Summer Camp* by J. B. Stine and J. Stine (Four Winds, 1981). This book offers a humorous treatment of camp life and deals with homesickness.

Being Lost: For four- to eight-year-olds, *Lost in the Store* by L. Bograd (Macmillan, 1981). Cute story of a boy getting lost in a department store, his adventures, and finding his parents.

Reducing the Fear

A common circumstance that arouses separation fear is when toddlers are with their parents in a large and crowded public place, such as in a department store or at the zoo.

Three-year-old Timmy had difficult separation problems in such places. He would whine, be cranky, and periodically insist on being carried—and he was getting too heavy for his mother to carry for long.

Why was his fear so strong? A year earlier, Timmy survived a car accident in which his father died. Since that tragedy, he and his mother Joan became very dependent emotionally on each other. During the first several months, they lived on some of the insurance money and were never apart. Then Joan got an invitation to move in with her parents so she could find a job. Grandma began to take care of him during the day while his mother worked. The daily separations were difficult for him and his mother, and she would telephone Timmy from work when she felt homesick for him. Their reunions each evening were highly emotional, and he would sit on her lap almost constantly.

Fortunately Joan decided to get psychological help for some of her own problems. From this process the therapist realized that the excessive dependency between Joan and Timmy had to be reduced. So he gave her some projects to work on with Timmy. One project focused on the boy's separation problems in department stores.

The first thing the therapist had Joan do was to put labels inside all of Timmy's shoes, giving his name, address, and phone number. Then Joan took Timmy to the shopping mall to teach him some relevant skills. They went when there were few customers, and they practiced what he would do and she would do if they got separated. For instance, two stores had centrally-located escalator-stairway systems that he could see fairly easily. She taught him how to find the stairs from different areas on each floor and showed him how she would look for him there as soon as she saw he was not with her. Joan also taught him how to ask a clerk for help and show the clerk the label in his shoe. All of this practicing was done initially with the mother close by and in view, and later with her gradually farther away and less visible.

Now Timmy was ready for counterconditioning of his fearful behavior in the mall. At first Joan arranged her shopping trips for times when the mall had few customers, and she had Grandma come with them. Grandma could help in two ways: she could provide some of the comfort that Joan usually gave and she could write down the progress Timmy made during the counterconditioning. The procedure they used had the following steps:

1. When Timmy asked to be picked up, Joan did so immediately and waited for a signal from Grandma that about 2 minutes had gone by. At that point Joan looked for a place to sit and said something like, "Boy you're getting heavy. Let's sit down for a minute." Timmy was seated between Joan and Grandma. After a while, they got up, Joan took his hand, and they began to walk. If he insisted on being picked up within about half a minute, they repeated this step.

2. Same as #1, except that Joan carried him for only 1½ minutes before sitting down.

3. Same as #1, except that Joan carried him for only 1 minute before sitting.

4. Same as #3, but Joan delayed picking him up by saying, "Yes dear. I'll pick you up in a second. Hug onto my leg while I look for a store." She stood there, looking around while silently counting 5 seconds. Then she picked him up for a minute before they sat down. As in the previous steps, they repeated this one if he asked to be picked up again within half a minute after they arose from sitting.

5. Same as #4, except that there were more customers at the mall (a moderate number of people, not a large crowd).

6. Same as #5, except that Joan carried him for only half a minute before sitting.

7. Same as #6, except that she extended the delay to 10 seconds before picking him up.

8. Same as #7, but within a few seconds of lifting him Joan said, "I'm so tired. I can't carry you. We'll have to sit down again." (It was during this step that Timmy did what they expected: he asked Grandma to carry him. She "tried," but put him down quickly, saying, "I'm not strong enough.")

9. The next time he asked, Joan said "I'm so tired now. But let's try something. I'll hold one hand and Grandma will hold the other one. And we'll all hold on really tightly. If you still want me to pick you up, we'll have to sit down again." The next time he asked, they sat down for a while.

10. Same as #9, except that there was now a large number of customers at the mall. Whenever he asked to be picked up, they sat down instead.

11. Same as #10, but Grandma said her hand was tired. She put a lollipop in the hand she had been holding.

12. Joan and Timmy went to the mall without Grandma at a time when there was a moderate number of shoppers. If he asked to be picked up, Joan said "You're too heavy for me now, but we can sit down if you're tired." She also praised and thanked him periodically for *not* asking to be carried. Just before they left the mall she bought him an ice cream cone as a treat "because you helped me a lot by not asking me to carry you, and I know that it wasn't easy for you to do."

The entire procedure took seven sessions at the mall to complete. Each of the steps had to be repeated at least once before progressing to the next one. By the time the procedure was done, he was showing some carry-over at home, being less clinging in the evenings. At that point Joan began to use some of the methods we considered for preventing and nipping the fear.

Day-Care or Early School Phobia

Beginning day care or school is a momentous event in children's lives. It represents an important and often sudden transition into a new "world." In that world children must be able to function separately and independently from their parents.

In Chapter 2 we saw that the emotional difficulty young children have when separated from their parents can cause *school phobia*. This is a fear in which children in the early grades may try to avoid attending school or become highly distressed while there. A similar problem can develop in children who are in day care. Although separation-related fear often shows up as soon as children start school, it can also begin after quite some time if they are feeling stress. This stress may result from the school situation, such as problems with teachers or classmates, or from the home environment, such as parental illness or the threat of divorce.

The initial separation when children start day care or school can be very stressful even if there are no serious problems at home. Because of the unfamiliar surroundings and people, most children feel at least a little uneasy at first, but they have the emotional strength to cope with these feelings. Once they do, they will discover that they can have a secure, enjoyable, and even exciting time in this new place.

Preventing and Nipping the Fear

Many parents have as difficult a time with the initial separation as their child does, especially if the child is starting day care. They worry that the child may not receive good care or may come to love the teacher more than the parents. If you have these worries, you may not do as good a job nipping the child's fears.

The best way to handle your worries about the quality of the care the child will get is to select the place very carefully. Visit several day care settings and make comparisons. Look closely at the facilities, play areas, and learning materials. Check the child-to-adult ratio—six children for each teacher or caregiver is very good. And look especially closely at the quality of the social interactions. Do the teachers and children seem trusting and friendly toward one another? Do they look each other in the eye? Do they smile at each other? Do the children and teachers initiate getting close to each other? Once you have selected a place and the child begins attending, maintain open communication with the child so you can detect problems in the making.

The second worry parents have is that their children will come to love the teacher more than them. Does going to day care or school disrupt the loving relationship children have with their parents? Many studies have been done to answer this question. Overall, the answer appears to be *no*. Children in day care continue to love their parents most, and this bond is not replaced by a relationship with the teacher or caregiver. Although these children develop an affection for an involved and stable caregiver in day care, "they still overwhelmingly prefer their mothers to this caregiver."[54] This conclusion seems to apply particularly to children who begin full-time day care after the first year.

Because attending day care or school involves both separation and meeting unfamiliar people, you'll want to examine the first two fears—of strangers and separation—covered in this chapter. If you have prepared your child for coping with these difficulties, you've made important inroads in preventing fears relating to day care or the early school grades. Additional suggestions are to:

- Maintain a positive attitude about the new world your child will enter, and convey this attitude to him or her.

- Familiarize the child with the place in advance. Take the child there on a weekend or evening to play in the yard, or just see "the place." Go again briefly when it is open to pick up an older sibling or neighbor child, or to see it in operation. Try to let the child meet the teacher and see the classroom shortly before attendance starts. Find out some of the games and activities your child will take part in during the first week or two. Do some of them at home.

- Take care of decisions and administrative details and paperwork in advance. This will reduce your own hassles on the big day and free you to make your child feel comfortable when the separation begins.

- If your child is starting day care, make transportation arrangements in advance and make sure they will occur regularly and on time. Many children will worry that their parents have abandoned them; don't give your child reason to form this worry by being late to pick the child up at the end of the day.

- If your child is starting kindergarten, determine how he or she will get there. Will the child walk, ride a bus, or be driven? Familiarize the child with the trip.

- If you have a good attitude about the child going and are prepared to "let go," accompany him or her on the first day. If you cannot feel confident in this role, try to have another familiar person do it. This companion should stay with the child for a while and encourage the child to take part in the activities. If the child has no difficulty, simply delivering the child to the classroom for the next day or two may be sufficient. If the child shows a little difficulty on the first day, the companion should fade out of the picture over the next few days.

- If you have any reservations about what you should do, consult with the principal, teacher, or caregiver. They've had a lot more experience than you have and should be able to give good advice.

If you expect that your child will have some trouble starting day care or school—the child is very shy or there are problems at home, for example—or if the child has begun attending and you notice some difficulty:

• Check with the teacher or caregiver immediately. They need to know what's happening with the child, and they can offer suggestions.

• If the child claims to be ill (see Chapter 2), check out the symptoms—with your physician, if you're not sure. If you decide that the child is feigning illness, take him or her to the day care or school as soon as possible.

• If the child is not ill, *do not discontinue attendance*— keep the child going every day. You must be firm and matter-of-fact about this, without getting angry. You should also make it clear that this issue is not open to discussion, debate, or negotiation. Why should you be so inflexible? Each time you give in to the child's refusal to go, you make the problem harder to correct. And if this continues, the behavior will become very difficult to reverse.

• Allow the child to take "security" objects to day care or school. A favorite doll or teddy bear can sometimes help.

• Permit the child to phone the parents occasionally, but keep a record of when and how long the calls occurred. Make sure this behavior tapers off, for instance by giving praise for not calling when the child gets home.

• Use the following books for bibliotherapy for children between three and six years of age. *All Ready for School* by L. Adelson (McKay, 1957) tells the story of a girl entering school with mixed feelings but finding that she enjoys it. *Shawn Goes to School* by P. Breinburg (Harper & Row, 1974) is about a boy who begins nursery school. *Will I Have A Friend* by M. Cohen (Macmillan, 1967) describes a boy's first day at school, initial loneliness, and finding a friend.

Reducing the Fear

If the problem has become chronic and entrenched, you may be in for a seige lasting several days. The most effective procedure is an extension of the previous suggestions. The parents of six-year-old Mary used the following method:

1. The issue of attending day care or school was not allowed for discussion. The evening before Mary resumed kindergarten her parents simply said, "Well, dear, tomorrow you go back to school."

2. For the first day back, her parents contacted the school in advance and worked out arrangements so the teacher was prepared. On the first morning, Mary's parents made sure she got dressed early. They gave her a light breakfast (to reduce nausea) and did not have a discussion about school. When she protested going and claimed illness, they took her temperature and said, "You may not feel well, but you're not too sick to go. Daddy will take you on his way to work." Any other protests were totally ignored, as if they weren't even happening.

3. At school, the teacher made special efforts to include Mary and make her day as comfortable as possible. Mary cried a lot in the morning and vomited once, but a teaching assistant was available to help comfort her. Near the end of the day, the teacher complimented her for the times when she was calm and gave her a favorite game to play. The school psychologist talked with Mary during the last 10 minutes, and her mother arrived and talked with the teacher before taking Mary home.

4. That evening the parents complimented her on being calm part of the time she was at school. They added, "I know most of the day wasn't very nice for you. But we think you were as good as you could be on your first

day back, and your teacher thinks so too. We're really proud of you. Tomorrow will be easier for you." There was no other discussion.

5. The next morning Mary tried just as hard to avoid going, but to no avail. At school, she cried for only an hour and was cranky most of the morning, but she didn't vomit. She even seemed to enjoy a little of the afternoon. Mary's teacher praised her improvement during the day and in the presence of her mother later. Both parents complimented Mary in the evening and again noted that the next day would be even better for her.

6. After several days, Mary finally showed no difficulty at home or in school. On the way home that day, she and her mother shopped for a party to celebrate Mary's effort and accomplishment.[55]

FEAR OF MONSTERS AND GHOSTS

Young children have vivid imaginations, which usually is a wonderful and exciting thing. But when the imagination manufactures fear, it's not so wonderful. In children's early years, they are prone to fears of imaginary creatures—monsters, ghosts, goblins, and witches. Their mental abilities have not progressed to the point that they understand very well the difference between real and nonreal things in their experiences. Monsters and ghosts are presented to children in scary forms, and this leads to fears that are among the most common of early childhood.[56]

Preventing and Nipping the Fear

As we saw in Chapter 6, the best way to prevent fears of monsters and ghosts is to watch for and restrict or modify experiences from TV, movies, storybooks, comics, and stories they hear. You can do a pretty good job of this by the simple word *no*. But remember that the child will have experiences that you can't monitor. Let the child feel comfortable talking to you about them. Modifying these experiences is a little more complicated than prohibiting them. Young children usually have some understanding of what make-believe is. It is important to make it clear that monsters and ghosts are make-believe. They are used in stories, TV, and movies, but they don't exist in real life.

Here are some suggestions for preventing fears of monsters and ghosts:

• Use "What if . . . ?" questions about imaginary creatures to stimulate open communication if you think the child has concerns about them. For instance, "What if Vicky heard a noise and thought it was a ghost? What would you say to her?"

• Pick out a not-too-scary movie with witches, ghosts, or monsters. Watch it with the child and play "Pick-out-the-make-believe-and-silly-things," as described in Chapter 6.

• Use appropriate children's books for bibliotherapy. For children between three and six years of age, *Clyde Monster* by R. L. Crowe (Dutton, 1976) tells a story about a frightened young monster who lives in a cave with his parents. For four- to seven-year-olds, *Chasing the Goblins Away* by T. Tobias (Warne, 1977) is about a boy who enlists his stuffed Brown Dog to help him chase away the goblins. *My Mama Says There Aren't Any Zombies, Ghosts . . .* by J. Viorst (Atheneum, 1974) is about a boy who decides that even though his mother makes mistakes she's right about monsters existing only in his imagination.

Reducing the Fear

Bobby's introduction to scary imaginary creatures came from TV when he was only two years old. He and his older sister were watching cartoons while their parents slept on a Sunday morning. Bobby was frightened by a mean witch, and his sister didn't help matters. She began to imitate the witch and showed him how the witch would swoop down and get him. In later shows and stories with monsters and ghosts, he always saw himself as one of the potential victims. The monster got its come-uppance at the end of the story, but Bobby never assumed he was like the hero who would leave the encounter unharmed.

By five years of age Bobby's fears of monsters and ghosts were a problem. Whenever he saw one of these creatures in a TV show or movie, he would cry and run away. During the Halloween season, he refused to get a costume or go trick-or-treating and he became very uneasy and clinging if he saw scary costumes in stores—which were almost everywhere. He had similar problems in preschool as his classmates prepared for trick-or-treating.

How did Bobby's parents help him overcome his fear? First of all, they began to restrict his experiences with imaginary creatures. They took control of the TV, paid close attention to the content of movies before he saw them, and stored all scary comics and books in the attic. Then they used a counterconditioning procedure with relaxation exercises. Because his fear was based on nonreal things, the procedure used *imagined* and *symbolic* (such as pictures) situations. They took the following steps:

1. They trained him to relax, using methods like those in Chapter 7. They started by having relaxation sessions each evening before dinner. After a couple of weeks when Bobby could relax well, they added relaxation sessions just before bedtime.
2. They introduced imagined situations at the end of the early-evening relaxation sessions by playing a game called "Let's Pretend."[57] The first couple of times, they used pretend situations without monsters or ghosts. For instance, they said: "Pretend you're a

tiny, tiny seed in the ground . . . Now you are beginning to grow. You sprout a little leaf up from the ground and you start to grow taller. . . . You are reaching with branches up to the sun. Show me how you rush toward the sun. . . . Now you're taking a bath in the rain, and the wind is blowing a little. Show me how the winds makes your branches move. . . . You are getting bigger and starting to look like a tree. . . . Now many years have gone by and you are a big strong tree. When the wind blows through your leaves, your strong trunk stands firm and still." The parents went through the game slowly, allowing Bobby to really get into "being" a growing tree.

3. They played "Let's pretend you meet the Cookie Monster" from *Sesame Street*—a monster Bobby liked—while he relaxed.

4. In the next Let's Pretend, Bobby "saw Rodney"—a ghost he knew from a picture book and was mildly afraid of, but Rodney was "far away."

5. Next, Rodney was riding a bike outside Bobby's house.

6. Next, Rodney was downstairs reading a book.

7. Next, Rodney sat in a chair in the family room while Bobby played nearby.

8. In the next Let's Pretend, Bobby "saw" the moderately-feared witch from Hansel and Gretel "far away."

9. Next, the witch was sweeping the sidewalk near Bobby's house with her broom.

10. In this step the parents switched to symbolic situations by using a Hansel and Gretel picture book from the attic. As in the previous steps, they presented the situations at the end of an early-evening relaxation session. The book was placed 6 feet away, opened to a large picture of the witch.

11. The picture of the witch was 2 feet away.

12. They used a picture of a monster Bobby was very afraid of, and placed it across the room in view.
13. The picture of the monster was 8 feet away.
14. The picture of the monster was 4 feet away.
15. Bobby could now hold picture books of imaginary creatures and flip through the pages.

His parents did a few other things too. They praised his efforts after every session. When he completed the counterconditioning steps, they talked with him about monsters and ghosts, noting that there are some who are very friendly. They asked, "Who's the friendliest monster?" and he said "The Cookie Monster. I like him." Then they played Let's Pretend in which the Cookie Monster sat beside him—and when Bobby "saw" a not-so-nice ghost, it ran away when it saw Bobby's friend, and they reminded Bobby that he knows how to make himself feel relaxed now.

FEAR OF DOCTORS AND DENTISTS

A survey asked teenagers which of a list of things "ever really frightened you." One of the most frequent responses was hypodermic needles.[58] Many people—especially young children—are afraid of the medical procedures of doctors and dentists. Because these fears are so common in children, psychologists have even developed formal measurement scales to assess fearful behavior in medical settings.[59] Fortunately only a small percentage of children show fear that is strong enough to disrupt treatment.

Medical treatments that require the child to be in a hospital, particularly for one or more nights, need to be handled with special care. Hospitals are big, busy places with unfamiliar and frightening apparatuses and procedures. Add to this all of the unfamiliar people and the frequent—sometimes total—separation from the parents, and we've got the ingredients for an intensely fearful experience. I described in Chapter 6 how you can help make it less so. In our look at how you can help the child cope with fears of doctors and dentists, I will focus on the office-visit situation.

Preventing and Nipping the Fear

Many pediatricians and dentists are much aware and concerned that their treatment can become a source of fear in children. They have tried to adjust their techniques to make the situation more comfortable. Some dentists provide relaxation and counterconditioning methods for fearful patients, and some pediatricians try to make the experience pleasant—one I've heard about even entertains his young patients with magic tricks.

There are many things you can do to prevent the child from becoming afraid of doctors and dentists.

• Before the child's first dental appointment, play "Dentist." You be the dentist who's going to "make sure the teeth are growing right and are very clean." Have assembled a bib, mouthwash to rinse, a spittoon (or nearby sink), some small spoons and toothpicks as dental "instruments," toothpaste, and a toothbrush (preferably electric—it's more like the drill).

• Since children begin going to physicians in infancy, you can't treat going to the doctor's office as a new experience. But if the child is to receive a new and potentially frightening treatment, you may be able to simulate it with the child or a doll as the patient. Try to simulate not just the procedure, but also tastes, smells, and sounds that may accompany it.

• Some dentists will allow pre-visits to the office before the child's first appointment. On the first pre-visit, take some toys with you and spend half an hour or so in the waiting room. Talk to the dentist and hygienist for a while where the child can see you and then introduce them briefly. If they have a trinket to give her (you could even supply it), so much the better. On the second pre-visit, have the child sit in the dental chair with the dentist there. Let the child experience a few simple things: raising and lowering the chair, putting on the bib, seeing a few of the "friendlier" instruments (the dental mirror is a good one), rinsing, and having air sprayed into the mouth. If you hear the sound of a drill operating in another room, tell the child "that's the sound this funny thing makes," while you point to the quiet drill in your room.

• What do you say if the child asks, "Will it hurt?" The best thing to do is give a truthful answer that doesn't say yes or no, because you don't know. So, say: "Going to the dentist doesn't usually hurt; but if he has to *fix* a tooth, it can hurt sometimes. If it does, it will probably only hurt a little or for a little while."

• It generally helps the child if you give an overview of the medical or dental procedures he or she will experience. But don't give a lot of detail, particularly distressing detail.[60] Describing some sensory experiences to expect is especially good, such as the smell of alcohol, the sounds of equipment, or the tingly feeling that the anesthetic gives. The play sessions described above did most of this.

• Young children undergoing medical or dental treatment usually cope better if one or both parents can be present. But the child may be better off without you there if you are fearful yourself, or if you will fret constantly. For instance, some parents say things like "Don't be afraid. It doesn't feel as bad as it looks" or "Don't squirm if it starts to hurt. That will only make it hurt more."

One more thing: try to think about how much you say and how you say it. Here's a good example of how efforts to prevent fear can backfire.

In Los Angeles the City Council had placed cards in the city elevators assuring riders that they should stay calm, since "there is little danger of the car dropping uncontrollably or running out of air" . . . A year later the cards had to be removed because of complaints from elevator riders that the message made them anxious. Apparently most people had not worried about these dangers until they read the card meant to reassure them.[61]

Some children seem uneasy or protest a little when at the doctor's or dentist's office, reflecting that some fear is present. You may want to help nip the wariness in the bud in the following ways:

• You can teach the child to think about pleasant images and scenes, or a song or poem *(Whistle A Happy Tune)*. This is a *distraction* technique that allows the child control over how much of the medical or dental treatment to experience.[62] A variation of the distraction technique I have used for many years is to create my own pain by pressing my thumbnail into my finger. I can pay attention to this pain instead of the hypodermic needle. And it doesn't seem to hurt very much, perhaps because I control it.

• Use the following books for bibliotherapy.

Dentist: For children between two and five years old, *My Friend the Dentist* by J. Watson et al. (Golden Press, 1972) tells about the treatment experienced by a boy with a reassuring dentist. For four- to seven-year-olds, *The Dentist and Me* by J. Schalebin-Lewis (Raintree, 1977) gives a straightforward nonthreatening account of a boy who has an examination and a girl who has a cavity filled. *Doctor:* For two- to seven-year-olds, *My Doctor* by H. Rockwell (Macmillan, 1973) gives a narrative of a boy's experience getting a checkup. For four- to eight-year-olds, *Doctors and Nurses: What Do They Do?* by C. Greene (Harper & Row, 1963) describes the daily routines of doctors and nurses, and stresses their friendliness. *Hospitalization:* For two- to seven-year-olds, *Jeff's Hospital Book* by H. L. Sobol (H. Z. Walck, 1975) gives a story of a boy who goes to the hospital for a relatively minor eye operation. It describes his experience from admission to discharge, his feelings of loneliness and worry, and the friendly and helpful staff.

Reducing the Fear

When Renee was almost three years old she had to be hospitalized twice for a series of tests. There wasn't any pain involved, and the illness was relatively minor, so everyone thought she'd sail right through with no problems. As a result, her parents didn't take off from work to stay with her during the day. But she became very fearful of medical treatment. Children younger than three who are hospitalized and separated from their parents for minor treatment seem to be prone to medical fears.[63]

Renee's parents noticed that she had become fearful at the physician's ofice, but they thought it would pass. They scheduled her first dental appointment, but she got sick. After some other delays, she had her first checkup following her fourth birthday. Renee had to be coaxed and cajoled to enter the examination room. During the procedure she squirmed, looked scared, and at one point began to cry and push the dentist's hands away. Fortunately the dentist was sensitive to the problem of children's fears and got the family some useful advice.

Before Renee's next checkup, her parents applied a fear-reduction plan that incorporated all of the methods for reducing fear that we saw in Chapter 7. The plan comprised the following steps:

1. The parents trained Renee to relax (see Chapter 7). Although at four years of age she didn't really master it, she could relax acceptably well after a few weeks.
2. At the end of a relaxation session, they had her imagine Spiderman climbing up the exterior wall to the

dentist's office and calmly receiving dental treatment.

3. The parents had Renee relax and showed her photographs of smiling children seated in dental chairs.
4. Renee relaxed and imagined these children calmly receiving dental examinations.
5. Renee relaxed and looked at photographs of some dental instruments for 5 seconds.
6. She looked at the photographs for 10 seconds.
7. She looked at the photographs for 20 seconds and then held them in her hand.
8. She visited the waiting room for half an hour with her mother and six-year-old brother, who was not fearful of dentists, and they briefly looked at an examination room.
9. Renee relaxed and imagined Spiderman calmly getting dental treatment, and then standing by while the dentist looked in her mouth.
10. She watched with her mother while her brother had a dental checkup (they did this only once).
11. Renee went with her mother into an examination room, sat in the chair, and practiced relaxing. She also imagined that Spiderman was there.
12. Same as #11, but the dentist came in, put a bib on her, and fed her some pretzel sticks—one of her favorite snacks. (They did this step once).
13. Same as #12, but the dentist showed her some dental instruments, had her rinse, and sprayed air into her mouth—to which she exclaimed, "Oh, that tickles. Do it again!"
14. Renee went for a full examination. She used relaxation and imagined Spiderman was there. All went smoothly. That evening the family went to an ice cream parlor to celebrate all the effort she put into overcoming her fear.

Renee was fortunate that her dentist understood about her fear. Some dentists think that a child who tries to escape treatment is simply being willful. As a result, they use "physical restraints and coercion such as blocking the child's mouth and sometimes also his nostrils with the hand or towel . . . in order to force the child to cease resisting. These tactics are likely to terrify young children."[64]

FEAR OF HEIGHTS

Many children develop a fear of heights in early childhood, and they don't seem to outgrow it very readily as they grow older. Being afraid of heights ranks among the most common fears in adulthood. In a survey of almost 2500 adults, more than 40 percent claimed to be afraid of heights, and it ranked as the second most frequently listed fear in the survey.[65]

The fear of heights is involved in many related fears, such as of bicycles, skiing, amusement rides, flying, tall buildings, stairs, and bridges. At least once a week on some very long and high bridges people attempting to drive across must be "rescued" by police: they either stop as they approach the bridge, realizing their predicament, and need to be escorted across, or they try to cross, panic when they reach a high point, pull their car to the side, and wait for help. You then wonder how many others anticipate their phobia and drive many miles out of their way to avoid the situation entirely.

Preventing and Nipping the Fear

Babies have their first experiences with heights when they are picked up by adults. Picking up a very young baby should be done carefully, slowly, and securely. There should be no abrupt movements while you hold the baby, and some of the holding each day should include caresses, eye-to-eye contact, smiling, and talking in a soothing manner. Babies who have "difficult" temperaments need more parental attention to these factors.

In the early months of infancy you can begin to introduce more casual types of holding and bouncing, especially while the baby is on your lap. Later you can gradually introduce swinging motions, and eventually you can even play games that involve tossing the baby gently in the air and catching him or her. Always watch how the child reacts to each new level of height.

Most infants begin to walk being led by the hand at around 9 months of age, and they need the freedom to explore and to try out their newly developing skills for getting about. You can help the child learn to walk and to climb—with little risk of fears developing—by guiding these activities. Make sure that if he or she falls there will be a soft landing onto a carpet, padding, or your waiting arms. Also note that babies who try to climb stairs generally find it easier to go up than come down.

At around two years of age most children can climb a flight of stairs in an upright position, either by holding onto a railing or someone's hand. A year later they can go up without support, alternating their feet for each step as adults do—but they still have trouble coming down with smooth, coordinated motions. It is during these early years that children are especially susceptible to accidents that involve falling. Usually these accidents are minor, but sometimes the child may suffer injury or considerable fright.

The fear of heights can be averted by some of the following techniques:

Ask the child to help you get things that are just a bit out of reach. You can lift the child at first. Then have him or her step onto a short, sturdy platform or stool to reach.

Play a game with the child that involves heights. For instance, use the caterpillarlike toy of coiled springs, called a "Slinky," that goes step by step down a flight of stairs. Play something like "Let's see if you can stop Slinky before he gets all the way down" by having the child stop Slinky at the first step, then the second step, and so on.

Take the child hiking, initially in areas that have mild slopes and no cliffs and then in steeper, more challenging areas.

Play a game of collecting and identifying leaves of trees. Pick the child up to reach for leaves.

Take the child to a playground where there are climbing apparatuses, such as a slide, monkey bars, and a jungle gym. Pick a day when there are only a few other children there. Help the child to use the equipment.

Play "Follow the Leader" games with the child, introducing increasing heights. Use familiar surroundings at first, such as home or playground.

Do some dream-analysis, "What if . . . ?" questions, and complete-the-sentence activities (see Chapter 6). Determine the extent of the fear and what the child thinks might happen. Try to correct any misconceptions, such as that the "teeth" on escalator steps will bite, by explanations and demonstrations.

Use appropriate children's books for bibliotherapy. For children in the four to seven age range, *Michael Is Brave* by H. E. Buckley (Lothrop, Lee, & Shepard Co., 1971) is recommended. The story is about a boy who overcomes his fear of heights to help another child. For nine- to eleven-year-olds, *Toby* by A. Wallace (Doubleday, 1971) provides an adventure story that includes one child helping another overcome his fearfulness of heights.

One other consideration should be added about fears of heights and falling. Sometimes a physical problem within the ear mechanism can produce feelings of dizziness and loss of balance. A medical examination may be advisable if the fear persists and the child complains of dizziness.

Reducing the Fear

Six-year-old Tony was always wary of high places, but his fear became especially acute when his family moved to the twentieth floor of a high-rise building in New York City. The bedroom he shared with his younger brother had a floor-to-ceiling window, and because the room was small they had bunk beds placed near the window. Tony, being older, was given the upper bunk. From this vantage point the view was spectacular, including the view *down*. It wasn't long before he began to avoid all window areas in the apartment, to protest returning home when he was outside, and to have bedtime and nightmare problems.

The methods Tony's parents used that enabled him to overcome his fear of heights consisted of counterconditioning, observational learning, and reward. They began by putting furniture (dressers, sofas, etc.) in front of all floor-length windows and the glass door to the balcony. The bedroom window was blocked off to the top with a 7-foot high bookcase. Counterconditioning included symbolic, imagined, and real-life gradual steps in which Tony

1. looked through a picture book showing children on chairs and ladders.
2. imagined standing on a chair away from windows at home.
3. imagined standing on the fourth rung of a 6-foot ladder far away from, but looking toward, the windows.
4. looked at pictures of the New York skyline.
5. climbed up and down a 6-foot ladder at home, not near windows.

6. stood near and looked out a closed second-story window that extended down only to about 3 feet from the floor.
7. looked out a similar window at the fourth story.
8. looked out a similar window at the eighth story.
9. stood 3 feet from a similar window in his apartment, looking outside.
10. stood near and looked out that same window.
11. went to bed with bookcase moved, exposing about 3 inches of the window height.
12. went to bed with 9 inches of the window exposed.
13. went to bed with 15 inches of the window exposed.
14. went to bed with the entire window exposed.

Observational learning was then used to get Tony out on the balcony. While watching others out there, he played inside with one parent who encouraged him to move closer and closer to the balcony door. Rewards were used by having a chart of his progress that he would help to update. Periodically his parents would tell him that he had reached an important milestone, and they would take him on a special outing.

Since the fear of heights can take so many different forms, as in fears of flying and bridges, the types of situations that constitute appropriate gradual steps can vary. You may want to consider such situations as:

Driving up and down hills, across small bridges, and near seashore cliffs with the family.

Going on escalators and elevators together.

Going on increasingly challenging amusement rides together.

Driving to an airport to watch people boarding planes and to see planes landing and taking off.

Using training wheels for the transition from tricycles to bicycles.

FEAR OF ANIMALS AND INSECTS

Another very common type of childhood fear that often continues into adolescence and adulthood is the fear of animals and insects.[66] Usually the person is afraid of a specific class of animals or insects, such as rodents, dogs, insects that fly and sting, or spiders. Some adults are so afraid of insects that they seal off their windows, vacuum and sweep twice a day, and feel uncomfortable outside that "pure" environment. Snakes, spiders, and rats or mice are among the least-liked inhabitants of this planet—in adult American thinking, anyway.

Preventing and Nipping the Fear

A child who is not afraid of commonly feared animals and insects is not likely to become afraid of uncommonly feared ones, such as sheep or butterflies. Here are some ways you can prevent fears:

• Try to show the child reasonably tolerant attitudes and feelings about animals and insects. Certainly you want to restrict what comes into your home and on your property, but this can be done in ways that don't arouse fear. For instance, although you don't want spiders or wasps in the house, you don't need to kill them. They are easily trapped by placing a jar over them and sliding a thin piece of cardboard underneath to serve as a top. You can then release them outside.

• Let the child know that most insects and animals (except domesticated ones) try to stay away from people. You can show this to the child by trying to approach a squirrel, a bird, or a bee outside. Only a few insects land on humans. They may be annoying, but they rarely hurt you.

• Play an alphabet game in which the child names an animal or insect for each letter. Use pictures if you can.

• Play a game in which each participant tries to act like

and sound like certain animals and insects. Use pictures if you can, and many children's records and tapes have animal sounds that you could play. If the child chooses an action that is aggressive or unpleasant, such as a bee stinging, discuss the pleasant things bees do, gathering nectar and making honey.

• Be watchful of what the child sees on TV and in the movies. Restrict those shows that give an exaggerated and excessively negative view of animals and insects. Make sure the child *does* see realistic portrayals.

• Take the child to a children's zoo or to petting farms. If the child shows any reluctance at approaching certain animals, handle the situation sensitively. And keep those animals in mind for the game you play.

When the child shows wariness toward animals and insects, try these methods.

• If the child seems a little frightened of dogs barking, explain that this is the way dogs talk. "They talk loud, but that's just the way they are. Some people talk loud too, don't they?" you can say. You may even have a novelty recording of dogs "singing"—there's one of dogs barking to *Jingle Bells*.

• Describe some of the good things that animals and insects do, such as serving as seeing-eye dogs, making honey, catching annoying insects in their webs, and pollinating flowers.

• Describe the animal's or insect's "family" and how they protect their young and their home. Point out similarities to human families. This is a good time to tell the child that "If you leave them alone, they'll leave you alone. They only try to hurt someone if they think the person will hurt them or their family."

• Teach the child how to approach, pet, and handle the animal, such as a dog. This might be done with a toy dog, or one parent could play the role of a dog while the other instructs. Explain how the dog might feel about the child initially and about being handled roughly.

• Teach the child to discriminate between animals and insects in your geographical area that can *seriously* injure and those that cannot. A good example is poisonous versus nonpoisonous snakes—one can usually tell the difference by a few simple signs. (Your State Agricultural Service or Forest Service can provide information.)

• Use the following books for bibliotherapy. For children between three and seven years old, *That Big Bruno* by S. R. Tester (Child's World, 1976) tells the story of a boy who is at first afraid of a large dog but later overcomes his fear. For five- to eight-year-olds, *I Can Do It by Myself* by L. Little and E. Greenfield (Crowell, 1978) tells about the self-reliance and courage of a young boy who encounters a barking dog. *Boo to a Goose* by J. Low (Atheneum, 1975) tells a story about a farm boy who loves all animals, and even insects, except for one. Gus the goose keeps chasing him. The boy eventually overcomes his fear and accepts the goose's attacks as something that Gus can't help doing.

Reducing the Fear

Because we've covered a detailed procedure for reducing the fear of animals (snakes) in Chapter 7, we'll focus on insects here.

At the beginning of the book I introduced you to a five-year-old girl named Jo who became fearful of flying insects. Jo's parents followed steps in which Jo

1. looked at pictures of butterflies, placed 5 feet away.
2. looked at pictures of butterflies close up.
3. looked at pictures of bees, wasps, and yellow jackets, placed 5 feet away.
4. colored pictures of butterflies with crayons in a coloring book.
5. looked at pictures of bees, wasps, and yellow jackets close up.
6. colored pictures of bees in a coloring book.

7. watched from the porch as her mother caught a butterfly, put it in a jar with a lid, and took the jar into their house.
8. watched her father read the newspaper and watch TV with the jar and butterfly beside him.
9. watched from inside the house as her father took the jar outside, opened it, cupped the butterfly in his hands, and gently released it.
10. watched her father catch a wasp with a jar, cap it, and bring it into the house.
11. watched her mother, father, and brother as they watched TV with the jar near them, but 10 feet from her.
12. same as #11, but the jar was 5 feet from her.
13. watched the jar and took one step toward it.
14. went with her family to the porch and watched her brother open the jar and let the wasp fly away.
15. stood 5 feet from a light in the house at night that had a moth fluttering around it.
16. stayed in a room with her father as a wasp flew freely, and walked to within 5 feet of it.
17. watched her father put a jar over the wasp, and then *she* approached, slid a piece of cardboard underneath, and helped her father carry the jar outside to release the wasp.

Jo was much less fearful the rest of that summer and only needed a little refresher the following June.

FEAR OF DARKNESS

Probably very few adults always feel perfectly calm and secure in the dark. Try walking alone in the dark outside house where there are no street lights—or better still, unfamiliar neighborhood.

Children generally experience pitch-black darkness all alone only at bedtime. They may feel fearful in the dark at two years of age because they're separated from the parents, and at older ages they hear noises or see images and think there are monsters or ghosts lurking. When children feel fearful in bed, they solicit the company of their parents who are big and strong and protective. Children accomplish this by getting their parents to come to them—such as by asking for a drink of water or by asking to join the parents in their bed. Neither is a good thing for parents to permit for very long, especially the latter. When children come into your bedroom, take them to their own room immediately. If they seem distressed, soothe them in their own bed for a while and leave. Dr. Spock describes ways to handle these situations.[67]

Preventing and Nipping the Fear

Because the fear of darkness often relates to fears of separation and of monsters and ghosts, you'll want to look at those sections in this chapter. If the child begins having a mild bedtime problem, here are some ideas to use.

Play blind-man's-bluff in which the blindfolded child must find and identify each of several people in a room.
Play hide-and-seek or hide-the-toy in a dimly lit room, preferably the child's bedroom.
Play "Find the . . .": you hide something fairly large, such as a stuffed animal, in the child's bedroom and he or she must find it alone in the dark.

• Use children's books for bibliotherapy. For children between two and five years old, *Close Your Eyes* by J. Marzollo (Dial, 1978) tells a story of a boy who has pleasant thoughts about kittens and other animals while going to sleep. For four- to seven-year-olds, *Benny Rabbit and the*

Owl by J. Low (Greenwillow, 1978) is about the bedtime fear that a little rabbit has. His father helps him overcome it. *What's in the Dark?* by C. Memling (Parents' Magazine Press, 1971) is about a boy who calms his own fears at bedtime. (Books suggested in the section on fears of monsters and ghosts may also be useful for the fear of darkness.)

Reducing the Fear

Gerri began having difficulties at bedtime when she was six years old. At that time her family moved into a larger house and she got her own room. Gerri and everyone else thought this was wonderful for the first few days. Then she started to notice noises that she hadn't heard in her old bedroom. Her parents didn't know this. Instead of telling them, she would lie in bed until they retired and then go to their room, act her pleasantest, and begin to chat. After a few nights her parents tried to stop this, but when she told them how frightened she was and tearfully begged them to let her sleep with them, they let her.

By the next night, Gerri's parents checked with a psychologist-friend and worked up a plan. They started by leaving her door open, put a 20-watt lamp in her room, and let her keep it on all night for two weeks. Each night one parent would sit with her for a while—initially, so she could point out the noises. The noises turned out to be from the heating ducts expanding and contracting. The procedure the parents followed consisted of these steps:

1. The parents explained the noises and showed her that thin metal makes noise when the temperature changes. They did this by leaving an empty ice cube tray in the freezer over night. The next morning they put it on the table after she sat down to breakfast. As it warmed, it made a snapping noise.

2. While they sat with her at night they trained her to relax (see Chapter 7).
3. The parents explained that using a light all night wastes electricity, especially a bright light. So they asked her to try to use less light, and substituted a 15-watt bulb. They also put a mini-light in the bathroom and in the hall. Her door was left open.
4. They began to spend less time at her bedside, letting her finish the relaxation exercises alone.
5. They substituted a smaller bulb.
6. They spent only a few minutes with her to tuck her in and get the relaxation started.
7. The parents removed the lamp and substituted a mini-light.
8. They removed the light from her room, but left the mini-lights in the hall and bath.
9. They told her that she could leave her door open or begin to close it more and more if she wanted to.
10. After a couple of weeks she closed the door.

NIGHTMARES

Lots of children have nightmares, at least occasionally. It's not unusual for bad dreams to occur once a week or so and continue at this rate for a few months. A couple of hours after going to bed, children may awaken from a nightmare, crying and calling for the parents. Although young children have very vivid memories of their nightmares, they usually describe these dreams briefly, such as "Bugs"; older children give more elaborate descriptions.[68] Happily, most of the dreams children have are not very frightening to them. Their dreams tend to reflect the circumstances, concerns, and interests of their waking lives.

Another sleep problem that *looks* to the parents like a nightmare is called a "night terror." A child having a night terror may scream or talk loudly and show intense fear for about 15 minutes. But the child (a) appears to be asleep or in a trance; (b) is difficult to awaken; (c) may be sitting up, walking around, or lying in bed thrashing about; and (d) if awakened, cannot recall what was frightening.[69] Because of these features, night terrors seem to be a lot like sleepwalking. Even though parents who see their child in an episode naturally feel distressed, they need not become alarmed. Children generally outgrow these episodes without any special treatment.

Children who have nightmares can benefit from efforts by the parents.

Preventing and Nipping the Fear

Children's nightmares derive from the experiences and fears they have when awake. Therefore the best way to prevent nightmares is to keep to a minimum those experiences that arouse fear.

Also keep in mind that young children tend to believe that their dreams are real events that happen outside of themselves under the control of others. For this reason you may find the dream-analysis method described in Chapter 6 helpful. When talking about dreams try to help the child understand that dreams happen in the mind under our own control. We create them. If a nightmare occurs, help the child reshape or reinterpret the dream to his or her advantage.

Six-year-old Ricky discussed his nightmare with his parents at breakfast. He dreamed a monster was chasing him. His parents had him close his eyes and imagine that he could see the monster a block from his bedroom window. As he did, they had him pound on the table and shout confidently, "Get out of here, you stupid monster. Go away and stay away. I'm bigger and stronger than you think." They had Ricky shout this several times and imagine that the monster got farther away each time, eventually disappearing.

Reducing the Fear

The most appropriate method for eliminating a strong or recurrent nightmare is to reduce the waking fear of that object. For instance, after Jo's parents helped her overcome her fear of flying insects (earlier in this chapter), she stopped having nightmares about bugs flying into her ears and stinging her.

FEAR OF STORMS AND NATURAL DISASTERS

When a natural disaster strikes, many people are affected. Homes are lost, children and their families are injured, and some die. The aftermath is extremely stressful, making even the "lucky ones" victims. Families are relocated with friends or relatives. Nobody talks of anything else, and the TV shows scenes of destruction almost non-stop. Part of the aftermath involves coping with the fears that develop.

Thunderstorms are less traumatic than disasters, but they can be very frightening to children and adults alike. Since the fear of thunderstorms is so common, we'll focus on this, also offering some tips on helping children after natural disasters, such as tornadoes or hurricanes.

Preventing and Nipping the Fear

Here are general suggestions for helping children cope after a natural disaster strikes.

Encourage children to help in cleaning up debris or in getting help to those in need.

Keep families together, if at all possible, to avoid adding separation worries to the other stresses. If relatives or friends are in the hospital, try to arrange visits by non-hospitalized children.

Give honest and realistic explanations of the disaster and answer children's questions forthrightly.

Use appropriate books for bibliotherapy. One example is *The Day the Hurricane Happened* by L. Anderson (Scribner's, 1974). It describes realistically the experiences of two children and their family before, during, and after a hurricane at their house on an island.

A good way to help prevent a child from becoming afraid of thunderstorms is to turn the storm into a game. Start this while the child is quite young—at, say, two or so. Have the child comfortable and warm on your lap, sitting at a window indoors. As soon as you see lightning, say, "Listen for boom-boom." When it sounds, say joyously, "There it is. Oh, boy. That's a good one" and hug the child tightly. If thunder happens when you didn't see the lightning, joke, "Ho-ho! They tricked us that time." Get the child involved, saying "boom-boom" too. Parents who are too fearful of storms to do this themselves can have someone else play the game with the child. Parental fears of thunderstorms are often communicated to the child.

If the child is already showing apprehension during storms, try to check the fear at the onset.

• Inquire at your local library or natural science institute (if you have one) and see if they show films that help children understand thunder and lightning.

• Give the child an explanation of how lightning and thunder happen. If the child is very young, you'll need to be a little creative in this. Some parents prefer to use a purely fanciful explanation: for example, angels are bowling in the sky—lightning happens when they get a "strike" and the wind blows when they dance for joy. An explanation that's a little closer to the truth is that lightning happens when two clouds rub together (like sparks are made), and thunder happens when the lightning hits something in the sky, like another cloud. The more accurate you can make the explanation the better. You'll also want to tell the child not to take shelter from a storm under a tree because sometimes lightning hits trees. (The books you use for bibliotherapy may also have explanations.)

• Use "What if . . . ?" questions, as in Chapter 6. Describe the good things that rain does. Use books for bibliotherapy. For children three to seven years of age, I recommend *The Storm Book* by C. S. Zolotow (Harper & Row, 1952). It tells of a boy who experiences a summer thunderstorm and becomes unafraid. For four- to eight-year-olds, *Michael* by L. M. Skorpen (Harper & Row, 1975) tells the story of a boy who overcomes his fear of storms.

Reducing the Fear

Seven-year-old Donna was always a bit apprehensive during thunderstorms, like her mother. Then, while on a camping trip in the summer, she experienced a storm with only the tent for shelter. She and her mother sat huddled together, her mother giving as much comfort as she could. After that trip, Donna's fear was much stronger. She became preoccupied with weather reports and insisted on watching the TV report each evening. During the remainder of the summer she would hide in her room whenever a storm occurred.

As the next summer approached, her parents wondered if she had gotten over her fear. They suspected she hadn't because of her continuing interest in weather reports. So they designed a plan which, as it turned out, Donna needed. A twist to this plan is that the father "directed" it so that the mother and daughter could *both* overcome their fears of storms. The steps they used were:

1. Before the storm season began, the family learned to do relaxation exercises together.
2. Father made a tape recording of the first thunderstorm so they could use the sounds later. (They put the microphone at an open window that was shielded from the rain.) During the storm they played *Monopoly* and had the radio playing at a moderately loud volume. Donna seemed tense when lightning and thunder occurred.
3. That night Donna and Mother did their relaxation exercises. Before the end, Father played the tape recording at a very low volume (setting "1" on the dial, where "7" was as loud as a real storm). The only light on in the room was a 20-watt lamp near Donna.
4. Same as #3, but the volume is at setting "2."
5. To reduce Donna's interest in weather reports, her parents started to reward her for turning the volume of the TV down more and more. They posted a chart in her bedroom showing her progress and put some money in a bank to save for a toy she wanted.
6. Same as #3, but at volume setting "3." Donna and her mother also imagined they could see the rain.
7. Same as #6, but at setting "5."
8. Same as #7, and Donna looked at pictures of storms.
9. Same as #8, but volume setting was at "7."
10. Same as #9, and Father flashed the overhead ceiling light (100-watts) on and off twice to simulate lightning.
11. Same as #10, but lights flashed 10 times.
12. When the next storm occurred, the three of them did the relaxation exercises. Donna and Mother seemed calm throughout.

During the course of this procedure, two other storms occurred. The family played a board game together and had the radio on, as in step #2, at those times.

FEAR OF THE WATER

How young can a child swim? Infants can hold their breath and make swimming movements while held on the surface or underwater for a short time; they are born with this as a reflexive or automatic behavior. But they lose this reflex during the first year. Children are rarely able to hold their heads up for air and learn to swim before the age of two. By three, children have little difficulty learning to swim.[70] This assumes that the child is not afraid of deep water, of course.

Preventing and Nipping the Fear

You can start to help a child be comfortable with water in infancy. Baths can be enjoyable for the baby, and they're great opportunities for the two of you to play together. You don't have to put a lot of extra time into it. There are many quick and easy things you can do to increase the baby's enjoyment, like letting the infant squeeze water out of the sponge, or find out how slippery soap is on the skin, or see that some things float. Two-year-olds enjoy filling containers with bath water and pouring it out, washing objects, and pushing floating objects along the surface of the water.

What can you do to help a wary child become accustomed to deep water? Here are some ideas.

Take the child to a shallow, fairly calm creek and go looking for rocks or other things in the water. Introduce the child to water very gradually. If this goes well, try a similar little adventure at the edge of a lake.

Play a game on the steps of a shallow pool that requires that the child "tag" the top step briefly with his or her foot. Use lower steps later.

Take the child to a shallow pool or body of water where age-mates are enjoying the water. Encourage the child to play with the others near or in the water. Stay nearby.

Provide training in swimming skills, either with the suggestions in Chapter 6 or by enrolling the child in a swimming program. The YMCA aquatics programs are excellent.

Reducing the Fear

Some wary children do not get a comfortable introduction to deep water, and their fear gets worse. Other children develop a fear after a negative experience in water. John's fear was the latter type. He enjoyed deep water right from his first contact with it. Like many children he never got training in swimming—he just imitated what he saw others do. His skills were adequate for his needs. Mostly, he liked pools to splash around in and cool off.

When John was eight years old, his family rented a beach house for a week. It was there that he swam in the ocean for the first time and had a bad experience. A large wave swept him under, knocked him about, and thrust him finally to the beach, coughing and gasping. Water was now a dangerous business for him. When they got back home, deep water in a pool became frightening too. John didn't have confidence in the adequacy of his swimming skills any longer.

John's parents discussed the problem with him, and they designed a plan together to help him overcome his fear. They carried out this plan in the following steps:

1. They went to a public pool together, and John watched other children having fun in the water while he played games with his parents. They were sitting 30 feet from the pool.
2. Same as #1, but sitting 20 feet from the pool.
3. Same as #1, but 10 feet from the pool.
4. John walked along the shallow length of the pool, 10 feet from the edge.
5. Same as #4, but 6 feet from the edge.
6. Same as #4, but 3 feet from the edge.
7. He sat with his father at the shallow end of the pool with their feet in the water. John's father dared him, "I bet you can't make as big a splash with your feet as I can." The boy accepted the challenge, and his father let him win.
8. They sat on the first step of the pool (shallow end).
9. They stood on the second step.
10. They stood together on the bottom of the shallow end of the pool (3 feet deep).
11. John treaded water at the shallow end with his father nearby.
12. John floated on his back at the shallow end.
13. John swam a distance of 10 feet along the shallow side, near his father.
14. He swam along the shallow side while his father sat on the edge of the pool
15. John enrolled at the YMCA in swimming lessons to improve his skills and an exercise program to improve his endurance.

FEAR OF DEATH

Death is a difficult topic for people in our culture to discuss and prepare for easily. We usually see this topic as morbid, unthinkable, and unspeakable. When we do talk about death, we use euphemisms. We don't say "He died." We say he "passed away," "succumbed to the illness," "expired," "has gone to the hereafter," or even "kicked the bucket." Part of the reason our cultural attitudes about death continue from generation to generation may be that we hide the topic from our children. Death is the ultimate unknown.

Most children are confronted at an early age with the death of something or someone they know. Often it is when a pet, a friend of the family, or a relative dies. When death occurs, how is it presented to the child? Adults usually try to "spare" the child the realities of death, saying things like "He's asleep," or "He's gone away." Using phrases that "sound better" may confuse the child and instill fears of harmless everyday events, like going to bed or going on a business trip.

Preventing and Nipping the Fear

There are many easy and casual occasions in early childhood when parents can help the child learn about the concept of death. One example is when the child comes across a dead animal, as little David's father describes:

David, at eighteen months, was toddling around the back yard. He pointed to something on the ground. I looked and saw a dead bird. . . . David then crouched over and moved slightly closer to the bird. His face changed expression. From its initial expression of excited discovery and later puzzlement, now it took on a different aspect: to my astonishment, his face was set in a frozen, ritualized expression resembling nothing so much as the stylized Greek dramatic mask of tragedy. I said only, "Yes, bird . . . dead bird.". . . . Every morning for the next few days he would begin his morning exploration by toddling over to the dead-bird-place. He no longer assumed the ritual-mask expression but still restrained himself from touching. The bird was allowed to remain there until greatly reduced by decomposition.[71]

A few weeks later, David found another dead bird. This time he showed a very different reaction. He tried to bring it back to life by gesturing for his father to put the bird in a nearby tree. It didn't help to explain to the boy that being placed in the tree wouldn't work. So the father followed the child's request and placed the bird in the tree. By doing this David's father could teach him something about the concept of death.

We saw in Chapter 2 that children's understanding of the concept of death changes as they get older. At first they think death is like living in another place. Between six and ten years of age, children gradually understand that death is final and involves an absence of bodily functions. The concept of death becomes pretty fully understood at nine or ten years when children recognize that death is an inevitable and final absence of life. It's important to keep this progression in mind when discussing death with a child.

Experts in child psychology and child care—psychologists, pediatricians, and educators—tend to agree that open and honest communication about dying helps to prevent children's fears of death, and offer some specific suggestions.

• Help the child understand that death results from physical causes. Many children believe that people die because "they were bad," as if they died as a punishment.[72] TV often conveys that message. Parents sometimes use the opposite idea when talking to a child about the death of a loved one: "God wanted your grandmother in heaven because she was so good." Neither the punishment nor the reward idea helps the child understand death.

• If a pet dies, discuss the death truthfully with the child. Let the child participate in the burial if he or she wants.

Grieving is not a pleasant experience, but it may be a very useful and "healthy" one.

- Encourage the child to talk about death and ask questions. Try to find out what the child feels and believes, and whether he or she needs reassurance. Children's concerns about death often relate to their worries about separation from the parents.

- Avoid using expressions[73] such as "You'll be the death of me"; "I'll kill myself if you get left back in school"; "I'll die of shame if you don't go to Sunday school"; "You're making me sick."

- Use children's books to teach the preschooler about the natural processes of change and death. Change in the life processes of plants and animals is portrayed in *The Growing Story* by R. Krauss (Harper & Row, 1947) and *The Bear Who Saw the Spring* by K. Kuskin (Harper & Row, 1961). Death in an undomesticated animal is portrayed in *The Dead Bird* by M. W. Brown (Addison-Wesley; Young Scott Books, 1938/1965). In this story, children find a dead bird, bury it with a ceremony, put flowers on the grave, and eventually go on to other things in their lives. *About Dying* by S. B. Stein (Walker, 1974) is an informational book that should be a shared-reading by the parent and child together.

When death strikes close to home, children naturally begin to worry about and question many things. Most preschoolers can understand only a simple and very concrete explanation. Let's look at some questions and useful answers that might transpire at the death of a four-year-old's grandfather.

Richie: Grandpa is dead?
Parent: Yes, dead. He is dead. He doesn't eat or breathe or talk or walk anymore.
Richie: Won't he play with me anymore?
Parent: No, dear. Only live people can play. Grandpa died. He can't play anymore.

Richie: Will he come to see us?
Parent: No. Only live people can come back.
Richie: But why? Doesn't he love us? Is that why he won't come back?
Parent: Grandpa loved us all very much. He didn't want to die and leave us. But everyone will die someday.
Richie: Will you die too?
Parent: Well, yes. But it probably won't happen for a very, very long time. We never know for sure when it will happen. But I'll probably live until you are grown up. Grandpa was my daddy and he didn't die until I was grown. Most people don't die until they get very old.
Richie: I wish he could come back. I'll miss Grandpa.
Parent: We all loved Grandpa. We'll all miss him.[74]

Besides having open and honest communication with the child, you can help check intense fears of death by using bibliotherapy. Many books are available for children of various ages.

• For children between four and nine years of age, the following books are recommended. *Nonna* by J. Bartoli (Harvey House, 1975) deals sensitively with the grandmother's death and provides good information for the young child. *Nana Upstairs and Nana Downstairs* by T. DePaola (Putnam, 1973) gives a simple and touching story of a young boy's grief at the death of his grandmother. *My Grandpa Died Today* by J. Fassler (Behavioral Publications, 1971) is about a boy who mourns his grandfather's death but can still play while others are grieving. *Annie and the Old One* by M. Miles (Atlantic Monthly Press, 1971) tells a sensitive story about a Navajo girl who trys to stop her grandmother from completing a rug she's weaving because the "old one" expects to die when it is finished. *The Tenth Good Thing About Barney* by J. Viorst (Atheneum, 1971) describes a boy's reaction to the death of his cat.

• For children between eight and eleven years of age, these books are useful. *Tell Me About Death: Tell Me About Funerals* by E. A. Corley (Grammatical Sciences,

1973) is a nonfiction but gentle account of aging and death, as well as funeral arrangements. Several other books have the death of an immediate family member as a main theme. Death of a sibling is in *The Half Sisters* by N. S. Carlson (Harper & Row, 1976). Death of the father is in *Growin'* by N. Grimes (Dial Press, 1977) and *There Are Two Kinds of Terrible* by P. Mann (Doubleday, 1977). Death of the mother sometime in the past is in *Sam, Bangs, and Moonshine* by E. M. Ness (Holt, Reinhart & Winston, 1966).

Perhaps the greatest stress a young child can suffer is the death of a parent. Usually the surviving parent is so caught up in his or her own shock and grief that the children's emotional needs are not adequately addressed. Many surviving parents say nothing at all to the children about the death; of those who say something, many provide fairy-tale accounts, like "Your Mommy's gone to sleep forever."

Often children show little sense of loss or outward grief when a close family member dies. Young children don't understand fully what death is, and this may account for their seeming lack of concern. Older children may be so confused and shocked by the tragedy that they are simply numbed emotionally. Their outward calmness should not be mistaken as a sign that they don't love the dead parent. Sometimes their grief comes out later, and sometimes it happens privately.

Reducing the Fear

One form that the fear of death can take is in a person's aversion to things relating to funerals. Jerry developed a strong aversion to cemeteries at eight years of age, shortly after his father died. His mother tried to shield him from grief by having him stay at a neighbor's house through most of the mourning. He attended only a brief viewing at the funeral home and the burial.

Thereafter, Jerry refused to return to the cemetery and began to react emotionally when he saw funeral activities on TV. They had a long and frank talk about his feelings and his father's death, and she apologized for the way she treated him during the mourning process. They designed a brief procedure to help him overcome his aversion so that he would be able to visit his father's grave—something he very much wanted to do. They used the following steps:

1. Jerry's mother trained him to relax (see Chapter 7).
2. At the end of a relaxation session, she had Jerry imagine seeing a cemetery.
3. They drove to the cemetery, parked some distance from his father's grave, and conducted his relaxation exercises.
4. Same as #3, and they got out of the car and walked to within 50 feet of his father's grave.
5. Same as #3, but 20 feet from the grave. Jerry then watched his mother put flowers on the grave and meditate for a short while.
6. Same as #3, but they both walked to the grave, held hands in meditation, and Jerry put the flowers they brought on the grave. Then she hugged him, and they cried—with part sadness and part joy.

FEAR OF SCHOOL (AFTER SECOND GRADE)

When school phobia develops after years of good school attendance, the cause is rarely worry about separation from parents. It is typically more complicated. Often the fear has accumulated over years of academic problems. These children have had enough of failure and are soured on education. Their self-concepts include a sense of intellectual inferiority.

Sometimes a fear of school develops in children who have

done well academically. The precipitating factor is usually a long-term stressful situation, such as parental illness or divorce. This kind of stress can disrupt children's study habits and concentration, in and out of the classroom. It can also reduce their motivation to try to do well. All of a sudden, they're getting low grades—and this compounds the problem.

Many children are unfortunate enough to have both a poor academic history and current stress in the family operating together. One of the effects that either of these factors can produce is *test anxiety*. This is the fear that people have at an exam that "I'm going to fail." Children who are very anxious during a test often find that the mind "goes blank," even for questions whose answers they know. This is debilitating, frustrating, and anxiety-arousing. This experience often results in children becoming more upset and less efficient the next time they study. At the next test, anxiety and performance are worse.

These children need help early, before the self-concept suffers too much injury.

Preventing and Nipping the Fear

Children need to develop a strong sense of competence and trust in themselves early on. Those who do can ward off a sense of inferiority later when they begin to compare themselves with age-mates in school. The suggestions provided earlier in this chapter for preventing fears of separation can apply. In addition:

Make sure the child has learned and uses good study skills and habits. Check with the teacher for information.

Maintain a positive attitude toward reading and intellectual pursuits, without giving the child the idea that academic success is *the* essential accomplishment for being a worthwhile and lovable child.

Maintain good communication with the child's teachers. Consult with the school psychologist or counselor if you suspect a problem.

Be concerned when the child does not do well, but be constructive. Avoid sarcastic or ridiculing remarks like "How come you can't do as well as Melissa? She's younger than you and she already knows her multiplication tables."

Watch for social problems at school. Does the child get along well with classmates? Is there any teasing or bullying? Has the child had a serious falling out with a close friend? These things can trigger a fear of going to school.

If the child is ill and out of school for a few days or longer, make sure he or she keeps up with lessons and returns to school promptly after recovery. Be especially watchful if the absence occurred because of an illness that started at school or an accident that happened there.

If the child begins to show apprehension about school, here are some suggestions.

Try to find out specifically what's troubling the child. Maintain open communication and use "What if . . . ?" questions (see Chapter 6).

Consult with the child's teacher.

Arrange for remedial or tutorial help, preferably by a professional. If you don't know the subject area well or cannot be "detached" about the child's progress (few parents can be objective and unemotional), get someone else to do it.

Check with the teacher to have a "study buddy" for your child—a student who is academically and interpersonally able to help.

Use appropriate books for bibliotherapy. For children between five and nine years of age, a useful book is *How I*

Faded Away by J. Udry (Whitman, 1976). It tells the story of a third-grader who feels ignored and invisible at school, but he learns to play a musical instrument and gains recognition there. For ten- to fourteen-year-olds, *But I'm Ready to Go* by L. Albert (Bradbury, 1976) is about a sensitive girl with a learning problem, and *The Faraway Island* by B. Corcoran (Atheneum, 1977) is about a shy girl who becomes afraid when entering a new school, but overcomes the fear.

Reducing the Fear

Ten-year-old Carol had generally gotten "average" grades in her subjects. Taking her report card home was a dreaded experience because her parents always seemed disappointed. They didn't actually say "you're dumb," but they asked why she couldn't do better in reading, writing, and spelling when she did well in other subjects, such as arithmetic and art.

In the fourth grade, the assignments in the "verbal" subjects became much more difficult, and Carol kept thinking "I can't do it." Eventually she became upset before all exams (except arithmetic), feeling that she'd get sick. Her teacher noticed the problem developing and contacted Carol's parents after she became ill at two tests.

The school psychologist counselled Carol and her parents on a broad array of topics to enhance her self-concept. He also helped them design a plan to reduce Carol's test anxiety. The plan included the following steps.

1. Carol's parents trained her to do relaxation exercises (see Chapter 7) at home.
2. After she mastered the exercises, she learned a brief version to practice at quiet or free times at school. It had three steps: she (a) took a deep breath, and let it

out, (b) told herself "Relax. Feel nice and calm," and (c) thought about a pleasant event for a few seconds.

3. They posted a chart in Carol's bedroom where she recorded the time she spent (a) reading "good" children's books from the library and (b) studying her difficult subjects. Seeing her own progress on the chart was the "reward" for reading and studying.

4. At home near the end of a relaxation session, the parents had Carol imagine attending a regular class meeting.

5. She then imagined hearing about someone else who would have a test the next day.

6. Next, she imagined her teacher announcing a spelling test in a week.

7. She imagined studying three days before the test.

8. She imagined the teacher describing all the material the class had to know in one more day.

9. Now she imagined studying the night before the test.

10. Next Carol imagined walking to school with a classmate and disagreeing on the spelling of one word.

11. They disagree on four words out of twenty.

12. They look up the words, and find that each student was correct on two of the words.

13. Carol imagined sitting at her desk waiting for the test to be distributed.

14. She imagined taking the test, miswriting words she knew how to spell, and rewriting them correctly.

15. Carol imagined that, after the test was over, she heard a classmate spell three words differently from the way she did.

When Carol took her next exam, she used her brief relaxation method whenever she felt tense. She noticed that she felt more comfortable during the test and felt she did better on it—and did.

Carol was fortunate that her difficulty was seen at a relatively early stage and help was available. For so many children school problems become part of an overall pattern of maladjustment, and they begin to miss school on a regular basis. They usually need professional treatment by that point.

SHYNESS: FEAR OF SOCIAL CONTACTS

One of childhood's saddest figures is the withdrawn and isolated child. Children who are very shy often have poor self-concepts. They see themselves as unattractive, too tall or too short, too fat or too thin, and less intelligent than their age-mates. They also see themselves as unpopular and rejected by others, and they think those "others" are probably "right" for doing so.

Some shy children see themselves as attractive, but they lack social experience and skills. When placed with socially sophisticated children, they are reserved because they don't know the games, a "good opening line," or other skill they can acquire. Their shyness is probably only temporary. A child with a strong self-concept will catch up quickly.

As children get older, their fears of rejection and not fitting in can become quite pronounced. Children who can't cope well with these fears and see themselves as socially or physically unattractive can suffer greatly. Late childhood and early adolescence covers a span of time when the peer group becomes a central focus and one's physical appearance comes under scrutiny—by oneself and by age-mates.

Shy children and adolescents can lead lonely, isolated lives and make few friends. Unless this pattern is overcome, their fears can impair their social and professional lives in adulthood.

Preventing and Nipping the Fear

Children who feel good about themselves and socially competent are not likely to be shy. Many of the suggestions in earlier sections of this chapter, especially regarding the fears of strangers and school, apply here too. They are designed to help children's self-concepts and social skills. Efforts to prevent shyness can begin in infancy and early childhood. Here are some further suggestions.

• Communicate your love to the child unconditionally— no strings attached. Many parents don't do this. They say "I love you" but really mean "I love you IF . . . " The *if* relates to the child's behavior: if you get good grades, if you obey me, if you make the Little League team, and so on.

• Give the child clear guidelines for appropriate behavior and discipline that are *not* attached to your unconditional love. You can say, "I don't like your stealing" without saying or implying, "Therefore, I love you less." Children who feel accepted and loved by their parents seem to have a friendly air of assuredness that others find socially attractive and inviting. In contrast, children who feel rejected by their parents carry a debilitating thought: "If my own parents don't like me, why should anyone?"

• Involve the child in social activities. Just the act of introducing the child to guests carries a special message: the child *counts*. Many parents introduce only adults.

• Some children are uprooted and moved often, due to changes in their parents' careers, for instance. These children need special attention paid to their social development.

If you see that the child does not mix well among familiar age-mates, and this seems to happen often, several methods can help.

Try to assess what the problem is. Maintain open communication and use "What if . . . ?" questions (see Chapter 6).

If the child simply lacks social experience with age-mates, enroll him or her in group activities, such as lessons in swimming, arts and crafts, or dance.

Invite children for little parties, and have them play organized games, such as: "What Can You Do With . . . (common objects)," "Tell Me A Story," "Tell Me A Riddle," or "What I Saw on TV." Make sure all children have something to contribute.

Use children's books for bibliotherapy. For children between four and eight years of age, *Fiona's Bee* by B. Keller (Coward, McCann & Geoghegan, 1975) is about a lonely girl whose kindness in rescuing a bee leads to her making friends. *The Shy Little Girl* by P. Krasilovsky (Houghton Mifflin, 1970) tells the story of a sad and shy girl who becomes more outgoing. *Plenty for Three* by L. Skorpen (Coward, McCann & Geoghegan, 1971) gives a story written in verse about a shy girl who declines to play with a boy and girl at first and later joins them. For nine- to twelve-year-olds, *The Faraway Island* by B. Corcoran (Atheneum, 1977) is about a shy girl who enters a new school. *Cider Days* by M. Stolz (Harper & Row, 1978) tells the story of a girl whose best friend moves away, leaving her friendless and shy. Later, she and another shy girl become friends.

Reducing the Fear

Lisa had always been described as "sensitive," "self-conscious," and "shy." At eleven years of age she had only two friends, twin ten-year-old girls who lived near her home. Although most people viewed Lisa as "average-to-pretty" in looks, she thought she was "ugly." She had become excessively concerned with the shape of her nose, which she thought was crooked; the small lobes of her ears, after some kids teased her by calling her "no lobes"; and her legs, which she thought were too skinny. Teachers liked her because she was obedient, pleasant, and a good student.

Lisa's parents had always hoped that she would "begin to blossom" as adolescence approached, but it wasn't happening. Then one evening Lisa tearfully announced that her two friends would be moving away. She said, "I'll never have friends again." A few days later Lisa's parents said they'd like to help her make friends and asked if she'd try a plan they could design together. She agreed. Her parents got some books and other materials about shyness from nearby libraries. Jointly they developed a plan with the following steps:

1. Lisa's parents trained her to do relaxation exercises (see Chapter 7).
2. They devised an activity in which Lisa listened to the conversations of her classmates and jotted down something to remind her of the topic. At dinner each weekday evening she described the conversations. Every week she would pick several topics to learn more about. For instance, one week she picked a rock singer, a TV show, a sport, and clothing styles. When she was ready, she discussed what she learned at dinner on a weekend. Her parents showed lots of interest and praised her efforts.
3. Lisa and her parents got ideas and information about hobbies and activities she'd like to know more about. They encouraged her to learn as much as she could with an eye toward picking two or three to try for a while. When she selected two, her parents helped her get started. One of them required lessons, for which the parents made arrangements.
4. At one dinner each week they played "Comedy

Show.'' Each of them had the assignment of finding and telling two jokes or funny stories that were appropriate for eleven-year-olds.

5. They taught Lisa some skills on starting and maintaining conversations: asking questions about the other person, giving compliments, and paying attention to what the other says. They role-played each skill.

6. Her parents gave her information about famous people, such as Carol Burnett, who describe themselves as having been shy in childhood.[75]

7. They had Lisa begin a diary of ''good things'' about herself—her appearance, ability, thoughtfulness, accomplishments, or things she recently did. Her parents encouraged her to show it to them if and when she wanted to. More ''public'' was a chart Lisa posted in her room, showing the number of new ''good things'' entered each week.

8. In the evening near the end of a relaxation session, the parents had Lisa imagine walking up to a shy classmate and saying, ''Hi. Did you see . . . on TV last night?''

9. Next Lisa imagined telling a short joke and the classmate laughing.

10. Then she imagined telling a funny story and the classmate smiling.

11. Lisa imagined meeting a shy classmate on her walk to school and talking with her the rest of the way.

12. Same as #11, but the classmate was a shy boy.

13. Same as #11, but the classmate was a fairly popular girl.

14. At school Lisa (actually) walked up to a shy girl and said, ''Hi. Did you see . . . on TV last night?''. That evening Lisa and her parents talked about how the other girl reacted.

Lisa's efforts at school continued to expand her social contacts gradually. When she felt comfortable enough, she joined a couple of organizations and began attending meetings. Moreover, her parents continued many of their activities and discussions with her to maintain her skills and their fine family communication.

FEAR OF PERFORMING: STAGE FRIGHT

Suppose a friend came to you and said, "I'm in charge of the program for a charity fund raiser for handicapped children, and I need someone smart and personable like you to give a speech and read a poem. Would you do it? Please? It's such a good cause." If this request would trigger a wave of anxiety and frantic thinking about how to get out of doing it, "join the club." It's a very large club. The fear of speaking or performing to an audience is one of the most common anxieties of adolescents and adults.[76]

Many people who perform or give speeches as part of their careers suffer a great deal of stage fright. This includes physicians who must testify in civil court proceedings, sales representatives, college professors, musicians, and actors. Here's an example:

When she was about 5 years old, actress Connie Sellecca remembers, and making her stage debut as a tap dancer, she took a tumble in the middle of the performance. She will never forget it. She hauled herself up and carried on with the show, then—when it was all over—broke down in tears. Her father stepped in, picked her up and plopped her on the piano so that everyone could see her crying. To this day, Sellecca says, she is terrified of performing on stage. . . . "I'm afraid I'll fall on my face—just bomb out. I don't think I'll *ever* be able to get on the stage."[77]

This actress became a TV star. She could do this because she appeared in taped shows *without live audiences.*

As we saw earlier in this book, you don't have to experience embarrassment directly to become fearful of performing. But just about every child makes some mistakes in front of others. Their ability to cope with these experiences depends on many things, such as their self-concepts, how others treat them when they make a mistake, and how often they have positive experiences performing.

Preventing and Nipping the Fear

Not every child will eventually want to become a stage actor. But being able to perform or speak before an audience is very important for many social activities and career directions. So many people smother their own abilities and talents because they cannot cope with "being on stage" in front of an audience.

There are many similarities between shy children and those who have difficulty with stage fright. Often a child is both shy and afraid of performing. The methods for checking shyness will also help the child cope with stage fright. Here are some additional ideas.

Let the child know that everyone makes mistakes and feels embarrassed when they happen. Share with the child some of your own blunders and those of entertainers (for instance, on the "bloopers" TV shows).

Point out that sometimes when people make mistakes it's because they didn't practice their performance. When the child is going to perform, as in show-and-tell at school, have the child practice it for you. Be sensitive when suggesting "improvements."

Put on neighborhood plays and talents shows. Having children perform in groups is a good way to start them out. Be sure to praise equally all of the children, pointing out specific things each one did.

Play a "Story Game" in which the child acts the parts of characters from favorite books or TV shows.

In late childhood you can play social games like Charades, which puts each person "on stage."

Reducing the Fear

Bill was thirteen when he realized that his fear of performing was interfering with things he really wanted to do. For instance, he had become quite a good guitar player, but he played only in his room by himself. Bill was also a good writer of stories, but his English teacher was the only person who had read any. When his teacher asked him privately if he would share one of them by reading it in class, he declined. She helped him come to realize how his fear was preventing him from growing.

Bill's parents got together with the teacher and school psychologist to design a plan to reduce his fear. This plan consisted of the following steps, focusing initially on being able to speak to an audience.

1. Bill's parents trained him to do relaxation exercises (see Chapter 7).
2. Toward the end of a relaxation session, the parents had him imagine being called on in class and giving a correct answer.
3. Then Bill imagined reading a sentence from a book.
4. Bill imagined watching a group of classmates make a short presentation without errors.
5. Then, only one student made the presentation. This student was the spokesperson for a group which sat beside her in the front of the room. Bill was one.
6. The last presenter made a minor mistake and no one reacted.
7. Bill imagined himself presenting a geography re-

port—being nervous at first, but relaxing away the tension and giving a good talk.

8. He imagined two classmates asking supportive questions he could answer.

9. He imagined that a student in the back of the room looked as if she was asleep. But instead of feeling his talk was boring, he thought, "She hasn't been sleeping well because her neighbors have been having loud parties."

10. Bill did his relaxation exercises, then read one of his own stories aloud. He tape-recorded his presentation, listened to it and took note of what he did well, saying, "That was good."

11. Bill's parents were present for his reading.

12. Bill presented the story in the classroom with only his teacher and his closest friend present. They gave him feedback, stressing those things he did well.

13. After practicing at home, he presented the story to his class and was fairly calm through most of it. (Some students spontaneously praised him later.)

Bill felt an enormous sense of pride in conquering his fear and being able to share his work. He tackled playing the guitar in public next, and succeeded with that too.

Epilogue

Although every child will develop some fears, coping with them is an important part of becoming a mature individual. The insights and techniques offered in this book can help you help a child be happier, suffer less fear, and become an effective person.

Reducing children's fears is only part of a broader intent I had in writing this book. It is my hope that when you apply the knowledge you've gained from it, you will also strengthen the mutual respect, understanding, and love between you and the child—and your relationship will flourish.

References

1. Rimm, D. C., & Somervill, J. W. *Abnormal psychology.* New York: Academic Press, 1977.
2. *(a)* Graziano, A. M., DeGiovanni, I. S., & Garcia, K. A. Behavioral treatment of children's fears: A review. *Psychological Bulletin,* 1979, *86,* 804–830.
   (b) Sarafino, E. P. Children's fears. In R. J. Corsini (Ed.), *Encyclopedia of psychology* (Vol. 1). New York: Wiley, 1984.
   (c) Sarafino, E. P., & Armstrong, J. W. *Child and adolescent development.* Glenview, IL: Scott, Foresman, 1980.
3. Sarafino & Armstrong—see 2*c* above, Chapter 11.
4. *(a)* Graziano et al.—see 2*a*, above.
   (b) Jersild, A. T., & Holmes, F. B. Children's fears. *Child Development Monographs* (No. 20). New York: Teachers College, Columbia University, 1935.
   (c) Sarafino—see 2*b*, above.
5. Sarafino—see 2*b*, above.
6. Sarafino—see 2*b*, above.
7. Bowlby, J. Separation anxiety. *International Journal of Psychoanalysis,* 1960, *41,* 69–113.
8. Rutter, M. *Helping troubled children.* New York: Plenum Press, 1975.
9. Hetherington, E. M., & Martin, B. Family interaction and psychopathology in children. In H. C. Quay & J. S. Werry (Eds.), *Psychopathological disorders of childhood.* New York: Wiley, 1972.

10. *(a)* Lonetto, R. *Children's conceptions of death.* New York: Springer, 1980.

   (b) Sarafino & Armstrong—see 2c, above.

   (c) Speece, M. W., & Brent, S. B. Children's understanding of death: A review of three components of a death concept. *Child Development,* 1984, *55,* 1671–1686.

11. Lonetto—see 10a, above, p. 154.

12. LeShan, E. *Learning to say goodbye: When a parent dies.* New York: Macmillan, 1976, pp. 14–15.

13. Jersild & Holmes—see 4b, above.

14. *(a)* Buss, A. H., & Plomin, R. *A temperamental theory of personality development.* New York: Wiley, 1975.

   (b) Chess, S., & Thomas, A. Temperament in the normal infant. In J. C. Westman (Ed.), *Individual differences in children.* New York: Wiley, 1973.

   (c) Thomas, A., Chess, S., & Birch, H. G. The origin of personality. *Scientific American,* August 1970, pp. 102–109.

15. Rutter—see 8, above, pp. 118–119.

16. Rutter—see 8, above, pp. 14 and 119.

17. Buss & Plomin—see 14a, above, p. 7.

18. Sontag, L. W., & Wallace, R. I. Preliminary report of the Fels fund: A study of fetal activity. *American Journal of Diseases of Children,* 1934, *48,* 1050–57.

19. Sarafino & Armstrong—see 2c, above, Chapter 3.

20. Watson, J. B., & Rayner, R. Conditioned emotional reactions. *Journal of Experimental Psychology,* 1920, *3,* 1–14 (quote from p. 5).

21. Sarafino & Armstrong—see 2c, above, p. 72.

22. Kempe, C. H., & Helfer, R. E. (Eds.) *The battered child* (3rd ed.). Chicago: University of Chicago Press, 1980.

23. Martin, H. The child and his development. In C. H. Kempe & R. E. Helfer (Eds.), *Helping the battered child and his family.* Philadelphia: J. B. Lippincott, 1972 (quote from p. 23).

24. Jersild & Holmes—see 4b, above.

25. Hagman, R. R. A study of fears of children of preschool age. *Journal of Experimental Education,* 1932, *1,* 110–130.

26. Venn, J. R., & Short, J. G. Vicarious classical conditioning

of emotional responses in nursery school children. *Journal of Personality and Social Psychology*, 1973, *28*, 249–255.

27. Zimmerman, B. J. Modeling. In H. L. Hom & P. A. Robinson (Eds.), *Psychological processes in early education*. New York: Academic Press, 1977.

28. *(a)* Parke, R. D., & Slaby, R. G. The development of aggression. In P. H. Mussen (Ed.), *Handbook of child psychology* (4th ed., Vol. 4). New York: Wiley, 1983.
    (b) Sarafino & Armstrong—see 2c, above, Chapter 10.

29. Graziano et al.—see 2a, above, p. 813.

30. *(a)* Brown, A. L., Bransford, J. D., Ferrara, R. A., & Campione, J. C. Learning, remembering, and understanding. In P. H. Mussen (Ed.), *Handbook of child psychology* (4th ed., Vol. 3). New York: Wiley, 1983.
    (b) Gelman, R., & Baillargeon, R. A review of some Piagetian concepts. In P. H. Mussen (Ed.), *Handbook of child psychology* (4th ed., Vol. 3). New York: Wiley, 1983.

31. Piaget, J. *The child's conception of the world*. London: Routledge & Kegan Paul Ltd., 1929.

32. Piaget—see 31, above, p. 94.

33. *(a)* Pines, M. Invisible playmates. *Psychology Today*, November 1978, pp. 38–42, 106.
    (b) Singer, J. L. *The child's world of make believe: Experimental studies of imaginative play*. New York: Academic Press, 1973.

34. Fraiberg, S. H. *The magic years*. New York: Scribner's, 1959, pp. 16–18.

35. *(a)* Pines—see 33a, above.
    (b) Singer—see 33b, above.

36. Bettelheim, B. *The uses of enchantment*. New York: Knopf, 1976 (quotes from pp. 7–8, 24–25, 41–42, 116–136).

37. Sarafino & Armstrong—see 2c, above, Chapter 11.

38. Bandura, A. Self-efficacy: Toward a unifying theory of behavioral change. *Psychological Review*, 1977, *84*, 191–215.

39. Sarafino & Armstrong—see 2c, above, Chapter 7.

40. Paul, G. L. Insight versus desensitization in psychotherapy two years after termination. *Journal of Consulting Psychology*, 1967, *31*, 333–348.

41. *(a)* Eme, R., & Schmidt, D. The stability of children's fears.

Child Development, 1978, *49*, 1277–1279.

(b) Gelfand, D. M. Social withdrawal and negative emotional states: Behavior therapy. In B. B. Wolman, J. Egan, and A. O. Ross (Eds.), *Handbook of treatment of mental disorders in childhood and adolescence.* Englewood Cliffs, NJ: Prentice-Hall, 1978.

(c) Graziano et al.—see 2*a*, above.

(d) Miller, L. C. Fears and anxieties in children. In C. E. Walker & M. C. Roberts (Eds.), *Handbook of clinical child psychology.* New York: Wiley, 1983.

42. Braga, J., & Braga, L. *Children and adults: Activities for growing together.* Englewood Cliffs, NJ: Prentice-Hall, 1976.

43. Stewart, K. Dream theory in Malaya. In C. Tart (Ed.), *Altered states of consciousness.* New York: Wiley, 1969.

44. Rubin, J. R. *Using bibliotherapy: A guide to theory and practice.* Phoenix, AZ: Oryx Press, 1978.

45. Braga & Braga—see 42, above, pp. 262–264.

46. Jones, M. C. The elimination of children's fears. *Journal of Experimental Psychology,* 1924, *7,* 382–390.

47. Hatzenbuehler, L. C., & Schroeder, H. E. Desensitization procedures in the treatment of childhood disorders. *Psychological Bulletin,* 1978, *85,* 831–844.

48. (a) Gelfand—see 41*b*, above.

(b) Graziano, A. M., & Mooney, K. C. *Children and behavior therapy.* New York: Aldine, 1984, Chapter 4.

(c) Hatzenbuehler & Schroeder—see 47, above.

49. Lazarus, A. A. *Behavior therapy and beyond.* New York: McGraw-Hill, 1971, p. 211.

50. Thelen, M. H., Fry, R. A., Fehrenbach, P. A., & Frautschi, N.M. Therapeutic videotape and film modeling: A review. *Psychological Bulletin,* 1979, *86,* 701–720.

51. Bandura, A., Jeffery, R. W., & Gajdos, E. Generalizing change through participant modeling with self-directed mastery. *Behaviour Research and Therapy,* 1975, *13,* 141–152.

52. (a) Agras, W. S., Sylvester, D., & Oliveau, D. The epidemiology of common fears and phobias. *Comprehensive Psychiatry,* 1969, *10*, 151–156.

(b) Graziano et al.—see 2*a*, above.

53. Berberian, K. E., & Snyder, S. S. The relationship of tem-

perament and stranger reaction for younger and older infants. *Merrill-Palmer Quarterly,* 1982, *28,* 79–94.
54. Clarke-Stewart, K. A., & Fein, G. G. Early childhood programs. In P. H. Mussen (Ed.), *Handbook of child psychology* (4th ed., Vol. 2). New York: Wiley, 1983.
55. Kennedy, W. A. School phobia: Rapid treatment of fifty cases. *Journal of Abnormal Psychology,* 1965, *70,* 285–289.
56. Sarafino, E. P. *Children's temperaments and the development of fears.* Paper presented at the annual meeting of the Eastern Psychological Association in April, 1983.
57. Braga & Braga—see 42, above, pp. 275–277.
58. Gallup, G. Phobias affect nine in ten teens. *Daily Intelligencer* (Newspaper), June 24, 1982, p. 21.
59. Winer, G. A. A review and analysis of children's fearful behavior in dental settings. *Child Development,* 1982, *53,* 1111–1133.
60. Miller, S. M., & Green, M. L. Coping with stress and frustration: Origins, nature, and development. In M. Lewis & C. Saarni (Eds.), *Origins of behavior* (Vol. 5). New York: Plenum, 1984.
61. Thompson, S. C. Will it hurt less if I can control it? A complex answer to a simple question. *Psychological Bulletin,* 1981, *90,* 89–101 (quote from p. 96).
62. Miller & Green—see 60, above.
63. Moore, W. T. (1975) Reported in F. Kent, *Nothing to fear: Coping with phobias.* New York: Barnes & Noble, 1977, p. 71.
64. Gelfand—see 41*b,* above.
65. Bruskin, R. H. (1973) Reported in F. Kent, *Nothing to fear: Coping with phobias.* New York: Barnes & Noble, 1977, p. 9.
66. (*a*) Bruskin—see 65, above.
    (*b*) Gallup—see 58, above.
67. Spock, B. *Baby and child care.* New York: Pocket Books, 1976.
68. Foulkes, D. Dreams of innocence. *Psychology Today,* December 1978, pp. 78–88.
69. Borkovec, T. D., Slama, K. M., & Grayson, J. B. Sleep, disorders of sleep, and hypnosis. In D. C. Rimm & J. W.

Somervill (Eds.), *Abnormal psychology*. New York: Academic Press, 1977.

70. Sarafino & Armstrong—see 2c, above.

71. Kastenbaum, R. The kingdom where nobody dies. *Saturday Review*, September 23, 1972, 33–38 (quote from p. 37).

72. White, E., Elsom, B., & Prawat, R. Children's conceptions of death. *Child Development*, 1978, *49*, 307–310.

73. Formanek, R., & Gurian, A. *WHY? Children's questions*. Boston: Houghton Mifflin, 1980, p. 132.

74. Sarafino & Armstrong—see 2c, above.

75. Zimbardo, P. G. *Shyness*. Reading, MA: Addison-Wesley, 1977.

76. Bruskin—see 65, above.

77. Warren, E. Many of TV's top performers are too insecure to enjoy their stardom. *TV Guide*, January 16, 1982, 37–40 (quote from p. 37).

Bibliography

Angelino, H., Dollins, J., & Mech, E. V. Trends in the "fears and worries" of school children as related to socioeconomic status and age. *Journal of Genetic Psychology,* 1956, *89,* 263–276.

Bauer, D. H. An exploratory study of developmental changes in children's fears. *Journal of Child Psychology and Psychiatry,* 1976, *17,* 69–74.

Blanco, R. B. *Prescriptions for children with learning and adjustment problems* (2nd ed.). Springfield, IL: Charles C. Thomas, 1982.

Coyle, P. J. The systematic desensitization of reading anxiety, a case study. *Psychology in the Schools,* 1968, *5,* 140–141.

Croake, J. W. The changing nature of children's fears. *Child Study Journal,* 1973, *3*(2), 91–105.

Fassler, J. *Helping children cope.* New York: Free Press, 1978.

Fensterheim, H. & Baer, J. *Stop running scared!* New York: Dell, 1978.

Fitzhugh, L. *The long secret.* New York: Harper & Row, 1965.

Ginott, H. *Between parent and child.* New York: Macmillan, 1965.

Knopf, I. J. *Childhood psychopathology: A developmental approach* (2nd ed.). Englewood Cliffs, NJ: Prentice-Hall, 1984.

Lang, C. Children's fears. In P. H. Mussen, J. J. Conger, & J. Kagan (Eds.), *Readings in child and adolescent psychology.* New York: Harper & Row, 1980.

Lewis, M., & Rosenblum, L. (Eds.), *The origins of fear*. New York: Wiley, 1974.

Maurer, A. What children fear. *Journal of Genetic Psychology*, 1965, *106*, 265–277.

Morris, R. J., & Kratochwill, T. R. *Treating children's fears and phobias: A behavioral approach*. New York: Pergamon Press, 1983.

Nagy, M. The child's theories concerning death. *Journal of Genetic Psychology*, 1948, *73*, 3–27.

Pomerantz, P. B., Peterson, N. T., Marholinii, D., & Stern, S. The *in vivo* elimination of a child's water phobia by a paraprofessional at home. *Journal of Behaviour Therapy and Experimental Psychiatry*, 1977, *8*, 417–421.

Quay, H. C., & Werry, J. S. *Psychopathological disorders of childhood* (2nd ed.). New York: Wiley, 1979.

Rey, M., & Rey, H. A. *Curious George goes to the hospital*. Boston: Houghton-Mifflin, 1966.

Rosen, G. *Don't be afraid*. Englewood Cliffs, NJ: Prentice-Hall, 1976.

Tasto, D. T. Case histories and shorter communications. *Behaviour Research and Therapy*, 1969, *7*, 409–411.

Wolman, B. B. *Children's fears*. New York: Signet/New American Library, 1978.

Index

for fear of storms and natural
disasters, 175
Boys, fears in, 21

Child abuse, 49–50
Communication between parents
and children, 98–108, 187
Conditioning
generalized, 47–48
gradual aspects of, 110–111,
114–117
in reduction of fears, 109–118
relaxation training in, 111–114
respondent, 45–47
Counterconditoning, 111–118
in fear of heights, 163–164
in fear of imaginary creatures,
152–154
in fear of separation, 143–144

Darkness, fear of, 18, 22, 33, 34,
83, 90, 168–171
bibliotherapy for, 169–170
case studies of, 77, 84, 170–171
prevention of, 169–170
reduction of, 170–171
Day care, 140, 145–148
Death
children's conceptions of,
29–33
fear of, 26, 28–29, 33–34, 73,
92, 179–185
bibliotherapy for, 182,
183–184
case studies of, 33,
180–181, 184–185
prevention of, 180–185
reduction of, 184–185
and separation anxiety, 28,
29, 33, 90
as monster, 29, 31–32, 33

telling children about, 29, 33,
35, 180, 181–183
Defense mechanisms, 72
Denial, 12
Dentists, fear of, 11–12, 118,
155–156
case studies, 11–12, 158–160
see also Doctors and dentists,
fear of
Divorce, 140–141
Doctors and dentists, fear of, 12,
34, 90, 154–160
bibliotherapy for, 157–158
case study of, 158–160
prevention of, 155–158
reduction of, 158–160
Dreams, 62–63, 100–101

Fairy tales, 66–68
Fearfulness, as personality
disorder, 13
Fire, fear of, case study, 114–116
Fraiberg, Selma, 64–65

Gender, as factor in determining
fears, 20–21
Ghosts, fear of, 14, 117, 150; *see
also* Imaginary creatures,
fear of
Ginott, Haim, 99
Girls, fears in, 21

Heights, fear of, 18, 34, 81, 90,
160–164
bibliotherapy for, 162
case study of, 163–164
counterconditioning for,
163–164
in infants, 160–161

DATE DUE

OCT 1 6 1986		
OCT 8 1988		
OCT 1 1 1988		
OCT 2 8 1988		
MAR 0 4 1992		
MAR 1 8 1992		
OCT 0 2 1993		
OCT 1 6 1993		
OCT 3 0 1993		
DEC 0 6 1993		
MAR 0 7 1994		
APR 1 1 1994		
MAR 2 0 1997		
APR 1 7 1997		
OCT 1 6 2003		
GAYLORD		PRINTED IN U.S.A.

WITHDRAWN